PRAISE FOR **UNFINISHED**

"Only time will tell whether AI, this latest in civilizational toys, will turn out to be more Gutenberg press or atomic weapon, but one thing is for sure: we will rely on voices of reason to shepherd us through the fog and signpost the journey. Using our world of film music as a backdrop, Lucas Cantor Santiago wrestles with some of the most pressing questions of our time. Lucas has carved a unique career for himself, operating at the frontier where technology and music meet, and has brought us a bounty of expertise and playful insight that makes for a fascinating read."
—ALAN MENKEN, EGOT winner and composer for films such as *The Little Mermaid*, *Beauty and the Beast*, and *Aladdin*

"In a remarkable mix of autobiography, philosophy, and technical detail, industry insider Lucas Cantor Santiago's *Unfinished* weaves a spellbinding account of what happened—and will happen—to the business of both capturing and creating music over the next sixty years."
—GEORGE DYSON, author of *Turing's Cathedral*

"If you're worried about what AI means for human creativity, read this book. It will make you feel better. Lucas Cantor Santiago has spent decades using technology to make art. In *Unfinished*, he shows us that music and technology have always evolved together, and he explains how that evolution will continue in the age of AI."
—JACOB GOLDSTEIN, host of the podcast *Business History* and author of *Money: The True Story of a Made-Up Thing*

"In *Unfinished*, Lucas Cantor Santiago reminds us that artificial intelligence is a tool, not a rival, empowering artists to push the boundaries of creativity while staying true to the human spirit. The future of art isn't about replacement; it's about reinvention."
—MANNY MAROQUIN, music entrepreneur and eighteen-time Grammy Award–winning mixer for Post Malone, Rihanna, and Kendrick Lamar

"Lucas is thinking about AI and music the way we all we should: with a mix of excitement, curiosity, and caution. In this super-engaging (and even funny!) read, I learned more about music, AI, and how an artist can harness AI for good."
—**DREW THURLOW, author of** *Machine Music: How AI Is Transforming Music's Next Act* **and former Senior VP of A&R, Sony Music**

"The world is full of theories about human-AI partnerships. Here you have a book—charming, surprising, illuminating—that goes beyond the certainties of theory to find the possibilities of practice."
—**ANGUS FLETCHER, author of** *Primal Intelligence: You Are Smarter Than You Know*

"Lucas Cantor Santiago has written a book about AI and music that is both timely and reassuring. He reminds us that new technology, from the primitive bone flute to Hans Zimmer's powerful computer rigs, has always enabled humans to create new sounds and invent fresh musical languages. This is an accessible and entertaining book fizzing with ideas and insights that should be read by musicians, music fans, and policymakers who want to understand the implications of AI for the future soundtrack of humankind."
—**LORD BRENNAN OF CANTON**

"The AI discourse is full of people who will explain it all to you without knowing the first thing about it. That's why Lucas Cantor Santiago's *Unfinished* is so necessary. Having used AI to finish Schubert's Unfinished Symphony, Cantor has learned about AI by doing, and his book reveals the strengths and the limits of the new technology more thoroughly than a dozen empty prophets."
—**STEVEN MARCHE, author of** *Death of an Author,* **the first AI-generated novel reviewed by the** *New York Times*

"As a researcher on the front lines of creative AI, this is the book I've been waiting for. Lucas Cantor Santiago's raw, honest journey shows how working alongside this technology allows us to find new sounds and make new meaning. *Unfinished* proves the ghost in the machine isn't something to fear, but a new kind of collaborator that amplifies our own creativity."
—**KORY MATHEWSON, artist and research scientist at Google DeepMind**

"This book is a major history and sociology lesson that I found fascinating and totally understandable. Thoroughly well-researched, it explains AI in a way that is completely new. Incredible in every respect."
—**M. B. GORDY, two-time Grammy-winning drummer, percussionist, and composer**

"An incredibly insightful and entertaining journey through the complex relationship between nascent AI technologies and contemporary music creation. The currently ubiquitous questions and concerns surrounding the future of human musicmaking in the age of AI are addressed and examined in virtuoso fashion through a whirlwind exploration of the age-old relationship between music and technology across millennia—with results that are both surprising and inspiring."
—**KUBILAY UNER, composer and director, Music Composition for the Screen MFA, Columbia College Chicago**

"Lucas Cantor Santiago brings a compelling and insightful perspective on the evolving relationship between music and technology, showing how they've been inextricably linked from humanity's earliest instruments to the sophisticated AI of today. It's a rich exploration of how we imbue sound with meaning and the ways that music might evolve in the near future. An important read for navigating the future of art."
—**MARK HENRY PHILLIPS, reporter (*Radiolab, All Things Considered*) and composer (*Serial, Homecoming*)**

"One of the eminent geniuses of our time explains it all for you, in a language all can understand."
—**LENNY BEER, Editor in Chief, *HITS Magazine***

"*Unfinished* inspires us to consider the deeply human experience of mastering our creative tools to tell the stories of humanity. Each act of creativity, whether made collaboratively with technology or despite it, contributes to our ongoing symphony of artistic endeavor—a piece that is, and always will be, unfinished."
—**MICHAEL STRICKLAND, Specialized Faculty in Music Technology, Florida State University**

"*Unfinished* cuts through both the hype and the hysteria to show us that music has always been a technological art form, and that technology amplifies rather than replaces the fundamentally human acts of creating meaning and moving an audience. This is essential reading for anyone trying to understand where music, tech, and AI actually meet—and why, at the end of the day, human musicians remain vital to our future."
—**CHERIE HU, Founder, Water & Music**

"An important and timely read for anyone curious about how our tools, from flutes to computers, have shaped what we call music. Exploring the complexities of human consciousness and creative expression, Lucas Cantor Santiago invites us to imagine AI not as a replacement for human creativity and skill, but as a tool that can help push us forward, expanding the future of composition."
—**MICHELE DARLING, Chair of Electronic Production and Design, Berklee College of Music**

"When reading *Unfinished*, one can start see a new conversation that is growing about the art of making music in the modern world. Lucas Cantor Santiago weaves a story of personal and technological epiphanies that will give some insight for all of us that are wondering what's next and what the future will hold."
—**DOM FLEMONS, "The American Songster," singer, songwriter, multi-instrumentalist, and Grammy Award winner**

UNFINISHED

UNFINISHED

THE ROLE OF **THE ARTIST** IN THE AGE OF **ARTIFICIAL INTELLIGENCE**

LUCAS CANTOR SANTIAGO

BACKBEAT BOOKS

Bloomsbury Publishing Inc, 1359 Broadway, New York, NY 10018, USA
Bloomsbury Publishing Plc, 50 Bedford Square, London, WC1B 3DP, UK
Bloomsbury Publishing Ireland, 29 Earlsfort Terrace, Dublin 2, D02 AY28, Ireland

BLOOMSBURY, BACKBEAT and the Diana logo are trademarks of Bloomsbury Publishing Plc

First published in the United States of America 2026

Copyright Lucas Cantor Santiago, 2026

All rights reserved. No part of this publication may be: i) reproduced or transmitted in any form, electronic or mechanical, including photocopying, recording or by means of any information storage or retrieval system without prior permission in writing from the publishers; or ii) used or reproduced in any way for the training, development or operation of artificial intelligence (AI) technologies, including generative AI technologies. The rights holders expressly reserve this publication from the text and data mining exception as per Article 4(3) of the Digital Single Market Directive (EU) 2019/790.

Bloomsbury Publishing Inc does not have any control over, or responsibility for, any third-party websites referred to or in this book. All internet addresses given in this book were correct at the time of going to press. The author and publisher regret any inconvenience caused if addresses have changed or sites have ceased to exist but can accept no responsibility for any such changes.

Library of Congress Cataloging-in-Publication Data

Names: Cantor Santiago, Lucas author
Title: Unfinished: the role of the artist in the age of artificial intelligence / Lucas Cantor Santiago.
Description: [1]. | New York: Backbeat Books, 2025. | Includes index.
Identifiers: LCCN 2025030032 (print) | LCCN 2025030033 (ebook) | ISBN 9798765143179 hardcover | ISBN 9798765143186 epub | ISBN 9798765143193 pdf
Subjects: LCSH: Cantor Santiago, Lucas | Schubert, Franz, 1797-1828. Symphonies, D. 759, B minor | Composers—United States—Biography | Artificial intelligence—Musical applications
Classification: LCC ML410.C32534 A3 2025 (print) | LCC ML410.C32534 (ebook) | DDC 784.2092—dc23/eng/20250801
LC record available at https://lccn.loc.gov/2025030032
LC ebook record available at https://lccn.loc.gov/2025030033

Typeset by Tom Seabrook
Printed and bound in the United States of America

For product safety related questions contact productsafety@bloomsbury.com.
To find out more about our authors and books visit www.bloomsbury.com
and sign up for our newsletters.

CONTENTS

INTRODUCTION • 1

I
Allegro
FROM MYTHS TO MICROCHIPS • 9

II
Andante
BIG QUESTIONS • 79

III
Scherzo
COWS, DNA, AND THE MAN OF
THE MILLENNIUM • 155

IV
Rondo
SAINTS, SIBYLS, SINNERS,
AND SYMPHONIES • 187

CODA • 225
ACKNOWLEDGMENTS • 235
INDEX • 239

I have the odd distinction of being the second-best writer and the second-best composer in my own family.

For Mami: For teaching me how to write

For Allison: For contributing as much to this book as I have

INTRODUCTION

WHAT IS THIS BOOK? WHO IS THIS GUY?
You've heard my work, even if you don't know that you've heard it.

I've worked in the television network music departments for every Olympic Games broadcast since Salt Lake City 2002, and I've won two Emmy Awards. My music has been featured in Super Bowl broadcasts, and it's been in the background of thousands of televised sporting events. I've played guitar, mandolin, mandola, banjo, bass, baglamas, charango, and percussion—and whistled—on hundreds of hours of music for major record labels, studio feature films, and network television shows. My music is performed regularly in concert halls around the world, and I tour as a lecturer on the topics discussed in this book. I'm an advisor and investor in many music technology startups.

I tell you all this, dear readers, to assure those of you who have never heard of me that the observations and ideas in this book are born of experience gained in the field the hard way, through trial and error. I'm not an academic, and this is not a textbook.

It's a book about music. It's a book about me. It's a book about those of us who have preserved the craft of music as players, composers, and listeners for the last 60,000 years. It's about the human race. And it might even be about what comes after.

I've loosely organized this book into four chapters to mimic the structure of a classical symphony from composers like Mozart, Schubert, and Beethoven. The form has served composers well for centuries, and it's the best way I know to connect many seemingly unrelated ideas and memorably convey thoughts and feelings. If we think of this book as a symphony, the first "movement," marked "Allegro" (meaning fast and upbeat) states the main themes and develops them a little to prepare the reader for the work and establish the tone. The second part of the book is the development movement, in this case marked "Andante" (meaning "slow" or "ponderous"). It introduces new themes and explores them in more depth, hopefully leaving readers relaxed but unsated and ready for the third chapter, which is marked "Scherzo," the Italian word for "joke." It's fast, punchy, and short, introducing a series of new themes that are each developed quickly before moving on to the next, leaving readers with the impression of brisk thoughtfulness garnished with a few memorable, clever turns of phrase. In this chapter, readers might feel like turning pages a bit faster. Its role is to set readers up for the finale: the last chapter mimics a "Rondo" ("round") movement in which key ideas are highlighted and brought to fruition, along with some new themes to provoke further contemplation.

INTRODUCTION

As the above suggests, astute readers will notice that I've woven themes from one "movement" into the next. These themes—like humans' continued attempts to understand the world through numerical abstraction—come up again and again, as do anecdotes about my brushes with a few famous people and many brilliant ones, people you will know by name and reputation. The opportunity to learn from these people prepared me to undertake the project that is the central focus of this book: in 2019, I finished Schubert's Eighth Symphony, the "Unfinished," with the help of artificial intelligence.

What does that even mean? If I finished it, what did AI do? If AI finished it, what did I do? These are complicated questions with, unsurprisingly, complicated answers. In the arts—and the sciences, too—how you try to find the answer is often more interesting than the answer itself.

For thousands of years, humans have contemplated the ideas in this book, wrestling with them even before they had written words to organize their thoughts. After all, the ability to think, as the name "Homo *Sapiens*" implies, is the very definition of our species. It's the differentiator between us and our primate cousins. Our thoughts led to written words, then printed words, then digital words.... Now, we have not only words, but machines that use words to help us remember and, in some ways, to think for us. You may well be reading this book with one of those machines, and the book itself was created on one of them—in this case, a MacBook laptop. In a relatively short period of time, evolutionarily speaking, we've evolved from the thinking man to the man who thinks with tools. The story of music can help us understand how and why we got here.

HOW DID WE GET HERE?

"Do you wanna drive it?" It was the fall of 2019, and Robert Playter, the CEO of Boston Dynamics, handed me the oversized remote control used to operate the Spot Robot, a piece of AI-powered hardware. Encased in yellow and black plastic, Spot walks on four legs and more or less resembles a headless dog. It looks menacing but is also kind of cute.

Spot is featured in YouTube videos doing choreographed dances to popular songs, but its official sales video is a long tracking shot of the robot walking through disasters, wars, construction sites, and factories filled with flying sparks. The implication is clear: you can use this very capable robot to do anything.

To say Spot sees the world as an abstraction would be misleading, because "seeing" implies an understanding Spot lacks. Spot's brain is a computer. Is it possible for a computer to be conscious? Or, to put it another way, is consciousness computable? You may think you know the answer, but it's still an open question.

To Spot, reality is no more than a collection of problems. When Spot is given a task, it uses artificial intelligence to identify and solve the problems that would otherwise prevent the task's completion. At least, that's the theory. Spot is not intelligent in the colloquial sense of the word, but it does seem to think—

INTRODUCTION

at least in the way an insect seems to think—as it navigates its surroundings. Despite the appearance of consciousness, Spot still needs a remote control.

Spot's controls are intuitive, and I probably could have learned to drive it in a few minutes if I'd been able to focus, but I could barely hear its maker's instructions over the chorus of John Legend's "All of Me."

Legend himself was performing about thirty feet away from us, strutting and gesturing as if he were performing for his customary endless sea of swooning fans. But we were at a private party on the lawn of a boutique luxury hotel in Pasadena, California. He was on a small stage built for the event with an audience of some two hundred of the world's top tech entrepreneurs and venture capitalists, none of whom were John Legend fans.

I was just beginning to have fun with Spot when its creator politely asked me to give back the remote. He wanted to demonstrate Spot for Masayoshi Son, one of Boston Dynamics' largest investors, and the CEO of the approximately $70 billion venture fund SoftBank.

Masa appeared to be in good spirits, which seemed odd considering that earlier in the week, the *Wall Street Journal* reported he'd lost $14 billion. SoftBank had been heavily invested in the company WeWork, which crashed as it tried to go public. The collapse was so spectacular, it later inspired a best-selling book, a documentary, and a biopic.

Evidently, losing more money overnight than most families

accumulate in several generations hadn't bothered Masa at all. His bearing suggested "you win some, you lose some."

I needed to give the CEO of Boston Dynamics space to talk to his lead investor, so I walked over to a couch where my wife, Allison, was enjoying the private concert and began to tell her about Spot, only to be interrupted by author and entrepreneur Arianna Huffington, a whirlwind of brilliance and charm. She wanted to tell me that she'd loved the piece of music I'd premiered earlier that day, which I'd composed with the help of artificial intelligence.

Allison looked at me as if to say, "How did we end up here?"

We'd been invited because someone at SoftBank heard that I'd finished Schubert's Unfinished Symphony by using artificial intelligence and commissioned me to compose something for the event utilizing AI. But Allison's look suggested something deeper. When we were children, artificial intelligence and robot dogs were science fiction. Now they were in the real world. How did we get here?

I began my music career as a luddite. Now I'd call myself a technophile. Technology won me over and has become an indispensable part of my creative process, as it is for most professional musicians today. If the idea that technology may be a permanent part of the art of music-making makes you recoil in indignant disgust, read on. This book is for you, and you may feel differently when you get to the last page. If you feel like technology is an important and maybe inevitable part of music's future, this book is for you too, and you may understand

INTRODUCTION

your own intuition a bit differently by the end.

Many readers, I suspect, believe as I used to that technology is moving too fast—that we are watching a revolution unfold. And in a way, we are. It is a revolution of process and of outcome, but it is also one of thought. Revolutions begin in the mind, and it is still up to us what shape this revolution will take.

When I began researching this book, I believed that new ways of learning music and creating it were "wrong," that technology was a threat to the very nature of art. I still believed this when I accepted the commission to finish the Unfinished Symphony with artificial intelligence, but I was too curious to say no. I still believed that technology was a threat to music when I drove the Spot robot at the Pasadena hotel after the premiere of my second AI composition, but I've always been slightly more curious than fearful, and curiosity has led me to the sometimes obvious, sometimes uncomfortable, and sometimes surprising realizations I describe in this book.

In researching and writing this book, I've changed my mind. And I've learned that the intertwined histories of technology and music have had only one constant for the entirety of human history: ongoing radical change.

Where did music technology come from? Where did artificial intelligence come from? And what do the answers to these questions mean for the past, present, and future of music, technology, and the arts?

When I began to work with artificial intelligence, I started asking these questions about the nature of my art form. Is it possible for a computer to think like a composer? Can a computer be conscious? What does technology do? Music exists in many forms, such as written notation and recordings, but what is it, actually?

This book is about questions I've been wrestling with all my life, questions that have led me down interesting roads. If you'll join me, I'd like to show you the way.

How did we get here? Let's start at the beginning.... Well, it's really the middle, but we have to start somewhere.

I

Allegro

FROM MYTHS TO MICROCHIPS

PYTHAGORAS

The fire raged with such intensity that its hiss and crackle drowned out any sound softer than a scream. The souls trapped inside realized that soon it would be impossible to breathe, and they would all die. But their lives didn't matter. All that mattered was that the teaching survived—that the Master survived.

In his past lives, the Master had been a fisherman, Apollo's female servant, and a Trojan war hero. Before reaching his current incarnation, he'd endured lifetimes of suffering. This minor tribulation, this burning building, this angry mob that didn't understand what he and his followers understood—all this was nothing compared to the magnitude of his knowledge.

The Master had founded a school at Crotone, and his teaching had already changed the world. Every one of his disciples would gladly die in service of the Truth the Master revealed. All the men trapped in the fire knew this as surely as they knew that the equilateral triangle was the most perfect of all shapes: the diagram of the universe and the basis for all numbers.

They traced the triangle—the sacred sign of their order—in the air with the precision of soldiers on maneuvers. Then, the Master's favorite disciple threw himself at the burning wooden wall, creating an opening that was quickly swallowed by flames. As if following a well-laid plan, the other disciples threw themselves at the wall, one on top of the other. Each one burned, each suffering as his skin was ravaged by the flames, and each perished slowly, in excruciating pain.

What little air was left became thick with the smell of burning flesh. But one by one, they created an escape from the inferno. The Master walked over the soft, warm bodies of his followers. The senior members of the order he had conceived, founded, and maintained for decades were smoldering beneath his bare feet as he walked into the astonished hands of his captors, who waited outside, still holding the torches they had used to set the blaze.

When the Master realized that all his followers were dead, he fell to his knees in grief, drew his last acrid breath, and died of a broken heart.

That is how Pythagoras of Samos died.

Well…it's one of the stories of how he died.

In another, he was pursued by an angry mob to the edge of a

bean field but refused to cross it because he believed that beans contained the souls of men, and to eat them or even disturb them was a sin. In this legend, Pythagoras, one of the foundational figures in the history of science, allowed himself to be beaten to death by a mob in service of a superstition about living legumes.

There are several other legends of Pythagoras's death, and what they have in common is that, in them, Pythagoras was teaching something so powerful that he attracted disciples willing to die for it. What he taught caused a revolution in thought so significant it provoked physical violence, and he was murdered by an angry mob. (The legends around Pythagoras also share many of the same descriptions of his beliefs about the relationship between men and beans.)

In his day, Pythagoras was such an important intellectual and cultural figure, it's impossible to separate truth from fiction in any detail of his life. He appears in the writings of Plato and Herodotus, and some of his own writings, known as the "Golden Verses," still survive and sound as true and prophetic now as they must have sounded when he spoke them two and a half millennia ago.

Pythagoras must have been what the author Jon Krakauer calls a "religious genius." Krakauer coined the term to describe the founder of Mormonism, Joseph Smith, but it could also apply to Scientology founder L. Ron Hubbard, or Jesus, or anyone who convinces followers that their ideas are more important than their individual lives. Pythagoras's religion is gone, but his legacy still haunts the pages of high school math books.

If you've thought about Pythagoras at all, it has probably been in connection with right triangles. High school students all over the world are taught his eponymous theorem, which describes how to derive the length of the hypotenuse of a right triangle from the length of its two sides: $A^2 + B^2 = C^2$. But his discoveries about triangles were just a small part of his life's work, which helped to set the stage for an intellectual revolution in Greece, the European Renaissance, and today's technological revolution. And like all great thinkers, he didn't get everything right.

Pythagoras's birth, so the story goes, was prophesied when his parents sought advice from the ancient oracle at Delphi and were told they would have a son who surpassed all other men in beauty and wisdom. The charmed, chosen child was born on the Greek island of Samos. When he was old enough, he traveled the world and was initiated into the secret wisdom of the Egyptians, the Babylonians, the Brahman Hindus, and the Caledonians. He learned philosophy and sophistry from the Greeks, then settled in the Greek port of Crotone (now in the Calabria region of Italy) where he founded his school.

Through his extensive learning, he came to believe that all knowledge could be derived from the sacred disciplines of mathematics, music, and astronomy. Pythagoras and his followers believed that the entire universe could be understood using the three disciplines in tandem, and this led them to study them with great fervor. Although his beliefs tended toward the mystical, his investigations into music were among the first recorded scientific experiments in human history.

Because Pythagoras believed that music was a window into the order of the universe, every sound was part of a divine symphony, and if we listened with open minds, we could gain a perfect understanding of reality. He called this divine symphony the "Music of the Spheres." One of his surviving Golden Verses is translated as, "The wind blowing, adore the sound." His followers would have understood this to mean that sound was one of the gods' ways of revealing their will through nature. The sound of the wind, the rhythm of a bird's flapping wings, the soft, sibilant speech you can almost hear in a babbling brook—each of these natural sounds was a means of communication used by the gods, and if we could just understand them, if we could just listen to them with love and adoration, we could know the gods' will and even understand their love for us. "Adore the sound."

"EVERYTHING IS NUMBER"

Even more so than his other aphorisms, Pythagoras's most famous Golden Verse is "Everything is number."

Pythagoras thought that everything could be represented in terms of numerical relationships—even the lives of animals and plants. He saw the universe in terms of a contemporary technology, the wax seals that were used to systematically certify commercial documents: he believed that each life-form was an imprint that was derived from a perfect seal created by a deity. Each copy was a little different, because each was individually stamped, but all imprints were recognizable as discrete instances of a single kind.

(About a hundred years later, Plato would modify and expand this concept. He described all creation as a mold imperfectly struck, like how each hand-struck coin was similar but not identical to the others of its kind. Both philosophers conceived of existence itself in terms of the commercial technology of their day.)

Pythagoras believed that man would eventually transcend his earthly body and exist as one with the perfect form created by the deity. In this state, man would be immortal; his soul would know everything and live forever.

The modern author, instrument builder, and Google engineer Ray Kurzweil also subscribes to this theory of omniscience and immortality through technology. He believes that a transcendent state will be achieved if we figure out how to upload our consciousnesses to a computer before our bodily deaths.

So far, these ideas remain entirely speculative. The human mind wants to believe that there is order in the universe that can be decoded and understood. Order is safety, order is security, and given the state of human knowledge at the time, Pythagoras's order must have seemed within the bounds of credulity. His followers thought he had truly discovered the Theory of Everything. We can hardly blame them, because we still want to believe in a natural order that contains the secret to immortality. Religious geniuses have always offered some form of eternal life and many of their followers have dedicated their earthly lives to the prospect of a better existence in eternity.

Before his forays into politics, Elon Musk was one of the

world's most optimistic techno-futurists. He has promised that his company, Neuralink, will make human-computer interfacing seamless by implanting something like a smartwatch directly into our heads. The idea is that a device will store your memories and personality, which can then be downloaded into a robot body.

Unfortunately, Musk is no closer to finding the key to eternal life than Pythagoras was. Like Pythagoras, he couches his theories in contemporary technology so they're comprehensible and seem plausible. No matter what we believe, everyone reading this book will eventually die. We may live longer than previous generations, but we won't live forever.

Sad as that may be, another of Musk's companies, Tesla, has made the electric car into a sought-after luxury item. Neuralink will not make you immortal, but because of Tesla, there are millions fewer planet-destroying, gas-fueled cars on the road. You don't have to get everything right to change the world.

Pythagoras was right about triangles, but he was wrong about the nature of the universe. In fact, Pythagoras was wrong about most things, but like Elon Musk and Ray Kurzweil, he changed the world anyway. Today, his worldview sounds like a quaint study in ancient superstition. But we still encounter many of his musical principles early in life.

I worked my way through college as a preschool music teacher. It was mostly silliness and fun, but between playtimes, I taught the children about pitch—the relative "lowness" or "highness" of musical notes—using colored plastic tubes of different lengths called Boomwhackers, which make discrete sounds when struck on the floor. You can buy them at any music store.

Messing around with these toys, I noticed that the big Boomwhacker marked "C," which produced the pitch C when struck, seemed to be exactly twice the length of the small one also marked "C," which produced a C an octave higher. You could play these two to get the first two notes of the song "Somewhere Over the Rainbow"—"Some" and "where"—which are a leap of an octave. A tape measure confirmed my observation that the small one was exactly half the size of the large one.

I didn't know this at the time, but I had repeated Pythagoras's observations about the relationship between length and pitch. I mentioned that Pythagoras performed some of the first recorded scientific experiments. By modern standards, they were so simple, any child (or preschool teacher) could do them, but in Pythagoras's time, testing things methodically and recording your results was a new technique.

Pythagoras measured the relationships between the lengths of strings and the pitches they produced when plucked. He was a musician himself and his experiments determined that pitches of plucked strings or struck objects had a predictable relationship to the object's size. The smaller the object, the higher the pitch. If you look at a set of Boomwhackers, you'll see that the high-pitched ones are shorter than the low-pitched ones. You can arrange them in a major scale simply by ordering them according to size.

Pythagoras's experiments were the beginnings of something

we've taken for granted for so long, it's difficult to imagine a time before it existed. They were early instances of written abstractions of the observable world. Abstraction is an incredibly powerful and useful tool in our cognitive toolbox. It allows us to use mental models, or even physical ones, as proxies for action in the real world. Abstraction allows us to think through complex situations with many variables and understand the likely consequences of the various possible actions without committing to a single, irreversible one. So, abstraction is a superpower, but it has a big weakness. Over time, we tend to confuse the abstraction with the actual object and make assumptions that are true of the abstraction but not true in real life.

French painter René Magritte illustrated this with a realistic painting of a pipe above the text *"Ceci n'est pas une pipe"*— French for "This is not a pipe." To paraphrase Magritte and take him one step further, you can't use a picture of a pipe to smoke tobacco.

IMPERFECT SYSTEMS

If you had been the first person in history to discover the relationship between size and pitch, you might think it was reasonable to conclude that all of nature could be described by similar mathematical ratios. Pythagoreans believed this, and this is why they saw music as a sacred way of understanding the connection between nature and number. "Adore the sound."

They believed that everything—the motions of the planets, human behavior, and even the transcendent and divine—could be described with equations and algorithms. They saw everything as a divine dance of vibrations. "Everything is number."

It's as obvious to a casual music fan as it was to Pythagoras that music contains patterns. Pythagoras believed that these patterns could be expressed as numbers, and, in some ways, he was correct. Readers who have an intuition that music and math are closely related are also correct, but that's only part of the story.

Twenty years after teaching pitch in a preschool classroom with Boomwhackers, I would find myself teaching artificial intelligence to recognize and reproduce the patterns of one of music's greatest geniuses, Franz Schubert. But what was I really teaching the machine? Was I teaching it to recognize and repeat some sort of musical law of nature? Was I initiating it into the mysteries of what Pythagoras called the "Music of the Spheres"?

Music and math are like a pipe and a picture of a pipe. Math can describe many important details about music, but many important things about music cannot be described mathematically.

When people are introduced to powerful mathematical truths like those Pythagoras discovered, they sometimes fall into the trap of ignoring seemingly minor inconsistencies, or trying to get natural phenomena to fit the abstractions that describe them. It's a bit like realizing that you can't smoke real tobacco with a picture of a pipe and trying to solve the problem with a picture of tobacco.

Western music—probably most of the music you've ever heard—is only one of the forms music took in its millennia-long

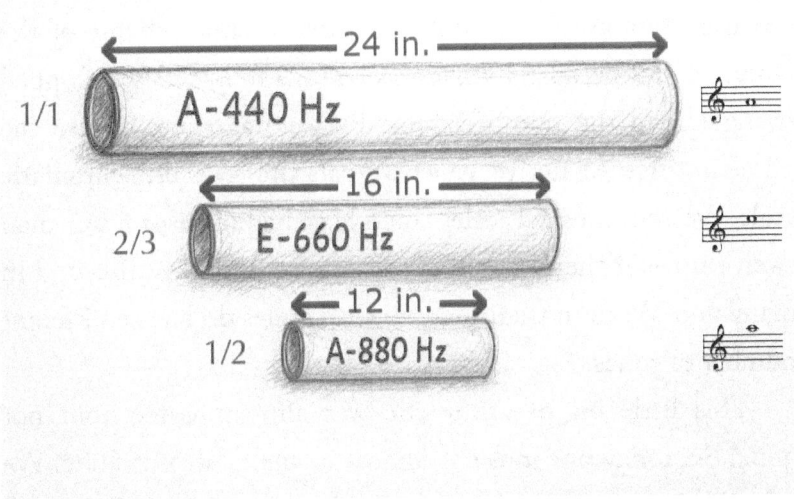

One of Pythagoras's most important legacies is the discovery that the pitch of a string, pipe, or other musical object is directly related to its length.

history. It took this form first because of, and then in spite of, Pythagoras. Through his experiments with sound, Pythagoras came to believe that certain ratios between notes, known as intervals, were more "perfect" than others. For him, this meant that their relationships could be expressed as simple fractions.

A violin string, or a Boomwhacker, that is two-thirds the length of another string or Boomwhacker sounds a fifth higher. (The interval is called a "fifth" because it's the distance between the first and fifth notes of a major scale.) If you take a string of any length and keep shortening it by ratios of one to three, you'll derive twelve unique pitches before you create one that has the same pitch as the one you started with, seven octaves higher than the original.

That's why the Western musical scale has twelve tones: not because there are twelve notes in some cosmic scheme of the Universe, but because Pythagoras and his followers worshipped triangles and the number three. Pythagoras chose to use the number three to derive what we call the Western chromatic scale. Western musical scales could have had more or fewer than twelve tones if they'd based the scale on something else, and in many non-Western traditions, musical scales do have a different number of tones.

This little bit of arithmetic was almost perfect, but not quite. So, today our music is almost in tune, but not quite. We have Pythagoras to thank for the fact that, in all likelihood, all the music you've ever heard has been out of tune in pure mathematical terms. For millennia, we have tried to ignore this inconsistency, but we still bend the real-world phenomenon to fit its mathematical abstraction.

Pythagoras's math and his insistence on a twelve-tone scale meant that each note in the Western chromatic scale has a slightly different interval between it and its higher neighbor than with its lower neighbor. This is a problem. Imagine trying to do an operation as simple as adding two plus two if the difference between one and two was slightly less than the difference between two and three. The fact that integers are equally spaced is fundamental to yielding meaningful mathematical calculations.

Rather than adding more notes or otherwise reconciling the fact that notes derived from two-to-three ratios are not evenly spaced, Pythagoras accepted this imperfection with religious dedication. Our modern solution is to prioritize even spacing between the notes, but we've kept the twelve-tone scale. As a result, our twelve notes are equidistant from one another, but some intervals are mathematically imperfect—and thus out of tune.

The intuition that a machine can never make music with the "soul" or "feeling" of a human being is confirmed by listening to fully machine-generated, mathematically precise music, and that's partly due to the built-in imperfection of our own system. We've grown used to the way these mathematically incorrect intervals sound. More on this later, but first, let's make your high school science teacher proud.

If you asked me "How far is New York from Los Angeles?" and I answered, "About six hours," it would be obvious that I was talking about flying in an airplane. But can you spot my mistake?

I've answered with the wrong units of measure. I was asked to solve a distance problem, but I expressed my answer in units of time. This "wrong" answer is so widespread, and so functional, it probably wouldn't bother anyone. But it bothers historians.

It's known as the problem of itinerant distance. Ancient texts often list a distance between two points as "three days' march" or "one day's walk." These measurements are an enigma to modern scholars. Armies don't march at uniform speeds, and road conditions can vary as widely from season to season as they do from one historical epoch to another. Contemporaries, who would have known how fast the king's army could march and been familiar with the topography and condition of local roads, would have found distance expressed as "days of march" just as useful as a distance of a few thousand miles expressed in "hours of flight" is to us.

In the ancient world, these cues would have been more useful than cues using exact time, because there was no exact time. The only reliable and universal measures of time were the day from sunup to sundown, the cycle of the moon, and the seasons.

Today, you can call someone in a remote part of the world and ask them the time. If they use an online clock like the one on your mobile phone, adjusted for time zone, they can tell you the exact time to the second. Because mechanical clocks cannot update regularly from a central server the way computer clocks can, this synchronization of time would have been unthinkable even a few decades ago.

Railroads allocated enormous resources to synchronizing time across just a few hundred miles of track. About two hundred years ago, before the railroads imposed their system, each town had its own local time. Neighboring towns could be minutes or even hours apart, which posed a big problem for creating train schedules. Splitting the continental United States into four time zones and enforcing railroad time at train stations was one of the railroad industry's solutions. Transportation technology created what we now take for granted as "time."

What does this have to do with Pythagoras or music?

We ignore problems that don't affect us, like itinerant distance. We also ignore problems that have been solved, however imperfectly. Time zones and radio-synchronized clocks solved the problem of coordinating time. Time could have been synchronized in any number of other ways. There's no universal law that says an hour has to be sixty minutes or that a day has to be twenty-four hours or that any of these measures need to be uniform. These divisions of hours and minutes were made arbitrarily thousands of years ago. (During the French Revolution, there was even a push to convert all forms of measurement, including time, to a system based on the number ten. The ten-hour day never caught on, but the other changes to the measurement of distance and weight are what we now call the metric system.)

The division of a year into 365 days is so imperfect, in fact, that we have to correct it every four years with the addition of an extra day, February 29. We could have made some days longer than others, but we prioritized the predictable periodicity of evenly spaced days of the same length, just as we prefer the periodicity of evenly spaced notes in a musical scale, although they are both approximations. We accept these solutions, no matter how odd they are, so long as they work well enough to keep our society organized.

The tuning of musical instruments combines two problems. Almost anyone, if they've given the matter any thought at all, assumes that instruments are tuned to notes that are somehow natural and universal. Those who know that this is not the case usually consider the problem of how to tune an instrument "solved" because instruments like the piano and guitar are built for the tuning system we've devised and gotten used to. We use math to describe the world, and when the world doesn't quite fit our descriptions, we adjust real-life phenomena so that it does.

But like railroad-synchronized time and itinerant distance, the tuning of a musical instrument, also known as its "temperament," is a very real problem. Most people don't think about it, and it hasn't been solved. The relationships between notes Pythagoras discovered were mathematically perfect but not evenly spaced, so we don't use them anymore. This is a problem for musicians and historians, and it's also a problem for NASA.

In 1977, NASA launched the Voyager mission, sending two unmanned probes into deep space. These probes have already left the solar system and will continue to fly away from the sun until they are either destroyed or found by another intelligent species. On board both Voyagers are identical Golden Records, which contain images, music, and sounds from around the globe, our way of sharing the sights and sounds of Earth with our distant neighbors. A beautiful and profound idea, I think.

Side one of the records contains music and sounds of various human activities and earthly phenomena like thunder, waves crashing, and a kiss. Side two contains what could be described as noise, but which can be decoded into images by using the transition frequency of the hydrogen atom as a universal reference. Scientists believe that this fundamental atomic property is constant throughout the universe and will be understood by any species advanced enough to capture our probe. NASA found an ingenious way to encode low-resolution images using sound, but the sound itself is heard as noise punctuated by periodic beeps.

FROM MYTHS TO MICROCHIPS

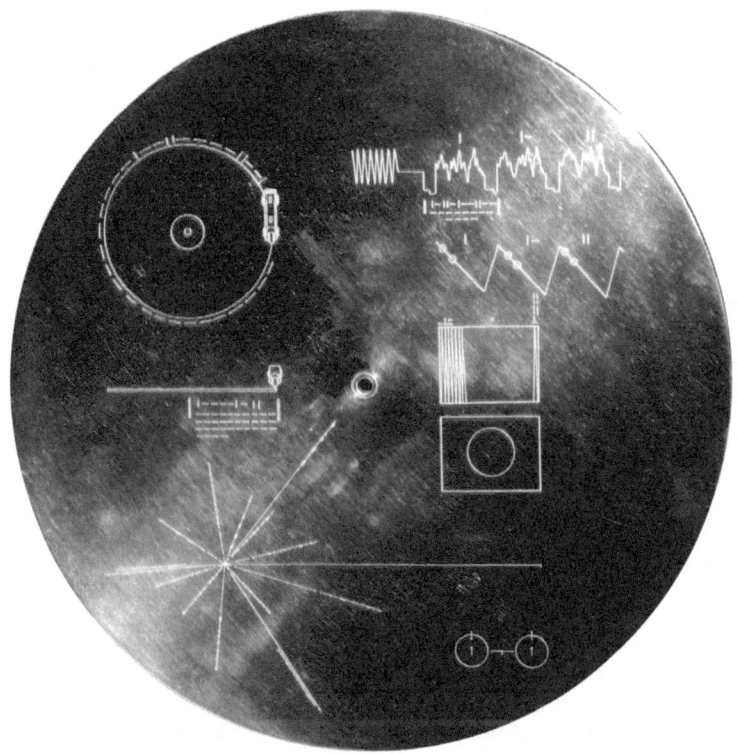

This diagram, included with the Golden Records on the Voyager spacecrafts, is intended to help an alien race access images that are encoded on the discs as sound. COURTESY NASA/JPL/WIKIMEDIA

The music on the Golden Record will probably also sound like noise to those who don't know its conventions.

Until the age of recording, instruments were tuned, or tempered, differently from one historical period to the next. Like time before railroads, temperament was regional. Tuning might be different from one town to another. Instructions on tuning, like itinerant distance, were based on local phenomena, such as a particular church organ, that might not be available as reference points for modern scholars. So how music sounded in the period before recording is largely unknown. Even when music is written down, the level of abstraction and reliance on convention is so great that only deep and meticulous scholarship can hope to uncover how even recent musical texts truly sounded. And it's always a learned guess based on deductive and inductive reasoning about what some markings on paper meant to the long-dead people who made them. We know that temperaments were different, but we don't always know which temperament was used when or where.

In our world of recorded music, electronic instruments, and modern guitars and pianos, we only know one temperament. We've known it for our whole lives—for several generations, actually—and most of us never know that other temperaments exist. As recently as a hundred and fifty years ago, Western music had different notes, notes we no longer use.

As I've explained, the chromatic scale in equal temperament—our current tuning system—is, in fact, out of tune. The fifths and octaves we're familiar with are perfect in the sense of preserving simple ratios, but other intervals like thirds and sixths are not, and these deviations are baked into the DNA of Western music. Even a non-musician can hear the difference between equal temperament and Pythagorean or "natural" temperament. It is very rare for Pythagorean temperament to be used, so while the music we hear is slightly out of tune, most of us have never heard an alternative.

FROM MYTHS TO MICROCHIPS

This fact is usually filed away as nerd knowledge, but some instrumentalists need to obsess about tuning due to the nature of their instruments. The decision on how to tune was made for us a few centuries ago by anonymous scholars who effectively mistuned our instruments for us. The only people who professionally think about this stuff are musicologists—students of the history and theory of music. Ross Duffin wrote a book on the subject called *How Equal Temperament Ruined Harmony*, a title so arcane he was compelled to add the subtitle *And Why You Should Care*. By now, you must be wondering, why *should* you care?

You should care because it's a commonly held belief that music is a direct and natural expression of human emotion. Yet music, especially contemporary Western music, is about as "natural" as the English language. Music is seen as a corollary of math, but its building blocks are a shoddy approximation of a simple mathematical concept, distorted for convenience. You should care about equal temperament because the music you've listened to all your life has been intentionally manipulated to fit the technology we use to perform it, from a shepherd's flute to a Fender Stratocaster. The tools we use have shaped the art form more than art has shaped the tools.

And you should care because in 1977, NASA sent a letter riddled with the mathematical equivalent of spelling errors into the universe and signed humanity's name to it. It's currently traveling away from the sun at about 34,000 miles per hour.

The aliens who find and play the musical segments of

the Golden Record, assuming they have some way to sense vibrations in the bandwidth of human hearing, are not likely to perceive the artistic sophistication behind what we've sent them. What they'll "hear" are imperfect relationships between frequencies of vibrating air. It will seem arbitrary and probably sound like grating noise to them. How could they conclude that there's content or art behind these relationships with no concept of human music and no indoctrination into its conventions and their meanings? They'll probably hear side two of the record—with its calculated noise and precise periodic beeps correlated with the energy in an atom—as more indicative of intelligence than the music side.

But if music is just arbitrary, made up, and out of tune, why does it move us so deeply?

THINKING IN LAKOTA

The Lakota language has no nouns. Its only parts of speech are what we call verbs. Everything in Lakota is relational, and the language cannot be spoken or understood without intuition and an inclusive understanding of all life. According to musician and radio host Tiokasin Ghosthorse, it is this intuition and the understanding of the relation of all things that cause Lakota language speakers to regard time or space completely differently from how we in the West view it.

In Lakota, everything is alive and everything is always "happening." This makes the language nearly impossible to translate. For non-Lakotas to understand it, the rich and complex concepts the language conveys must be reduced to mere nouns, stripping the timeless concepts and feelings of their meaning and firmly anchoring them in the Western concept of time. It's like reducing a burning, smoking, aromatic pipe to a mere picture of one. Tiokasin describes this process of translation as "taking a living feeling and 'nounifying' it to death."

Tiokasin's way of seeing the world is fundamentally different from mine, but we've been friends for twenty years and played meaningful and engaging music together. Our performances begin with Tiokasin in full regalia explaining the meaning of his Lakota names. After this long but engaging introduction, we improvise for as long as an hour. Tiokasin's clothing and his hypnotic voice speaking in Lakota position the audience for something otherworldly. Our concerts have an air of sacrament.

Offstage, Tiokasin is a scholar. When we're deep in discussion, he'll sometimes pause mid-sentence and say that English is a prison or that a specific idea can be expressed in a single phrase in Lakota, while in English, it would take hours to explain. How do I, a monoglot, respond to that? If English is a prison, I'm stuck in it with no hope of release. Worse, I don't even know what freedom is.

I can't verify this. I don't speak Lakota, and according to Tiokasin, it would be impossible for me to learn it at this point in my life. So, I'm doomed to live in a reality I only partially understand, while people like Tiokasin have a different and perhaps more robust understanding of the universe. But how could it be otherwise?

All our minds are prisons from which we can never escape. We privilege our own viewpoints and our own cultures, but other cultures and viewpoints exist, and we can't know them all. Each culture understands the complexity of the universe in its own unique and incomplete way. By its very nature, any language reduces reality to abstract forms, intelligible only to those who speak it. So, any language can only partially describe the universe. Because an abstraction is necessarily incomplete, the limitations of each language become the limitations of the minds who use those languages to express their thoughts and make sense of their surroundings. We are blind to things and concepts our language doesn't permit us to express.

When Tiokasin and I first began to play music together, I was most impressed by his flutes. He makes them himself from wood he gathers on the Pine Ridge reservation in South Dakota. His flutes are the length of his arm, and the distances between the holes are variations of the widths of his fingers. Each flute is a unique instrument with only one master, but they all produce tones easily represented in Western music. Their different pitches make up what Westerners would recognize as a scale—specifically, a "pentatonic" scale, which has five notes to each octave.

Tiokasin doesn't think about scales or keys or harmony when he plays, but he knows how to make the flute sound beautiful. I was in music school when we first played together in a working band, and all the latest music theory was fresh in my mind. I could recognize a tonality he was playing and use an unexpected harmony to make it sound any way I liked. Tiokasin reacted musically to these changes, and I reacted to his reactions. We were communicating in two different languages, each manipulating sound with no common intellectual understanding of what the other was doing, but the result was very pleasing to our ears and to the ears of our audiences. We used different abstractions to manipulate the same thing.

Tiokasin and I think in different languages. These languages, and the thoughts they allow us to formulate, are so different that we view one of the most fundamental aspects of reality, the passage of time, in completely different ways. Our minds are tuned to completely different and possibly incompatible models of the nature of the universe, yet the medium of sound makes these models mutually intelligible, and we can play beautiful and emotional music together.

Musicians can make music that is understood by an audience even if we don't understand it ourselves. If Tiokasin understands what I do only through his lens, and I understand what he does only through mine, is it a leap to imagine music created by a performer—a machine—who pleases an audience but understands nothing and simply executes notes and sonorities in an order they've learned by deductive and inductive reasoning? I don't think it is.

Music, like all arts, is shaped by feedback. Musicians learn what works and keep doing it, whether or not they know *why* it works. If an audience responds to a musical idea, and then a different audience responds to the same thing, we keep it in the show and call it experience, or wisdom, or showmanship. It's learned by trial and error.

Artificial intelligence running a Long Short-Term Memory (LSTM) model—an ancient AI technology by today's standards—works in a similar way. It tries options and receives feedback from a user, gradually "learning" trends and extrapolating conclusions from its new knowledge. This AI model of the universe is different from mine and from Tiokasin's. But it can make music, too: an LSTM is what I used to finish Schubert's Unfinished Symphony.

What does it mean that artificial intelligence can write a symphony, a feat most humans can't accomplish? What does it mean about humanity and technology and who we are and how our brains work? What does it mean for understanding what music is? If AI can write a symphony, is there anything it can't do?

After I finished Schubert's Eighth Symphony using artificial intelligence, these questions haunted me. In the years of reflection since, I've come to realize that the most obvious questions about technology, meaning, and the arts are the wrong ones to ask. Those questions have more to do with the portrayal of artificial intelligence in the media than with its actual or theoretical capabilities.

If human performers are just taking cues from an audience in the way an artificial intelligence takes cues from a user, how are we able to imbue the music we create with meaning? The ability of an artificial intelligence to make music that moves and inspires us has less to do with the AI than it does with the humans who hear it.

FROM MYTHS TO MICROCHIPS

In English, things happened, are happening, or will happen. In Lakota, things are always happening. To an artificial intelligence, time is not relevant at all. The AI exists in a universe of complete abstraction. The base layer of its reality is binary code, represented as electric charges on a silicon transistor. But artificial intelligence can already generate music we find acceptable. Calling a piece of music "acceptable" is hardly an inspiring description, but as far as we know, until now it's only been humans that can make any music at all.

We say that birds "sing" and whales communicate with "song," but this is verbal misdirection, a poetic application of the verb "to sing." What these and other animals do is more like speaking. We call these vocalizations "songs" because they often consist of discrete pitches in the same frequency range as our music. The wavelengths of whale songs can travel very far underwater, and the songs of birds can travel very far in a forest. These calls likely evolved because they're loud and intelligible over long distances, not because they are beautiful. But animal song interpreted through human ears is probably the beginning of our musical history.

Technology has been a part of music since the first time humans performed it. The oldest musical instrument on record is a 60,000-year-old flute fashioned from a bone. Why a flute? No one knows for sure, but archaeologists indulge in speculation to explain the origins of artifacts, and so will I.

The pre–Ice Age forests of northern Europe must have been loud. Bird calls, animals moving through trees, and the rustling of wind-blown leaves would make it difficult to distinguish the sound of birds from the sound of a flute, unless you knew what you were listening for. If your tribe had developed a simple language of whistles and pitches, you could easily recognize discrete notes in a certain order, but to anyone else, human or animal, the melodic language would be no more than another sound in the cacophony. Non-human animals, even other primates, are unable to determine if a series of notes goes up or down, so an instrument that could make bird-like pitches in any order would be the perfect tool for covert communication between humans over medium distances outside the line of sight.

A prehistoric flutist could sit in a tree or on a hill and relay information about the position of game or other humans to her clan-mates on the ground. A flute could have been an encrypted communication device used to coordinate hunting and warfare. Compelling evidence for this includes the fact that, in addition to its artistic career, the flute was used to coordinate war efforts until the nineteenth century. So, in the unforgiving prehistoric wilderness, the precious raw materials and time it took to make a flute would have been worthwhile.

A Neolithic flutist would have learned to be very adept at making sounds with the instrument, especially if she spent all day playing it to direct a hunt or any other activity. The life of her tribe might depend on her skill. She may have also used these skills to entertain the clan after the hunt was over.

In other words, it's possible that music originated as a primitive form of encrypted communication and evolved into entertainment. It may have served the dual purpose of entertaining and conveying information, as it still does, and relied on technology and cognitive capabilities no other animal possessed, giving humans a distinct advantage.

Imagine sitting around a campfire while a Neolithic musician played the flute and a shaman told the story of your tribe, possibly a tale that taught moral or practical lessons, as well as the tribe's living, shared history. The shaman might be subject to interjections, collaborations, asides, maybe even heckling from the people who witnessed the events in the story. In this scenario, music-making would have been a total collaboration, molding a new song with a moral purpose into a fixed form with easy-to-remember details that could pass information across generations.

Techniques would develop along with language to describe those techniques. Knowledge of the best materials for instruments and best practices for working those materials would be passed from one musician to the next and refined over millennia. The result would be a robust language of sounds spoken with tools—instruments—as well as finely developed technical language to describe the sounds. Music, the technology to sustain it, and a cultural understanding of its significance could easily have sprung from the desire to communicate basic information with the melodic contours produced by a bone flute.

When I began to play, music study was personal and lonely. It can take years of solitary practice before a musician develops the skills to tell stories with sounds. And I learned about this ancient collaborative approach to music not by studying anthropology but by working in the largest and most prolific film music production studio in the world. My journey from jazz guitar player to composer good enough to work at a studio like that began when a living legend invited me to see how a recording session worked.

TANGLED

You *love* Alan Menken's music. He wrote the songs and scores for Disney's *Beauty and the Beast*, *Aladdin*, *The Little Mermaid*, and too many other classics to list, along with hit musicals like *Little Shop of Horrors* and *Leap of Faith*. He's an EGOT winner, which means he has won an Emmy, a Grammy, an Oscar, and a Tony—some of them multiple times. You can almost certainly sing one of his songs from beginning to end.

Alan lives close to where I grew up. I went to school with his daughter, and he's a family friend. Before I moved to Los Angeles, I lived in New York City and worked as a music administrator and associate producer for NBC Sports and Olympics. One of my clients gave me access to a studio I could use after hours, and I created music for plays, commercials, indie films, and sports television. I had a degree in jazz performance but wanted to get serious about composition, so I reached out to the most successful composer I knew, and I was able to set up a phone call to ask Alan for advice.

We spoke briefly. I told him where I was in my career, and he invited me to come out to L.A. and attend one of his recording sessions. I was surprised he didn't have more to say, but I was flattered by the invitation. Alan was about to record the score to a Disney film called *Tangled*. I didn't know what to expect, but as soon as I got off the phone, I booked a flight.

For the past few years, I'd basically been living in a New York recording studio, and I thought I knew most of what there was to know about the process. I'd won an Emmy for working in the music department of the Beijing Olympics, and I was using that credit to get paying—low-paying—jobs.

I learned a lot from those projects, but now that I have many years of working at a high level under my belt, I can admit that my operation in New York was far from professional. Alan probably sensed this when we talked and thought the best thing he could do was to show me how the professionals do it.

I thought the difference between my music and Alan's Academy Award–winning, million-dollar scores was just budget, and that if I had access to a large orchestra and a world-class studio, I could make amazing, unforgettable music, too. It's embarrassing to admit that I discounted the role of genius, craft, and experience that were so obviously the differentiators between my music and that of a master like Alan. He could say more with a piano in a few minutes than I could with an orchestra and a month of preparation.

I didn't know what I didn't know. I was embarrassingly, confidently ignorant. I think young artists benefit from a certain amount of misplaced confidence, but I may have had a bit too much.

When I arrived in L.A. for the first time, I was welcomed

by a dreamlike familiarity that seemed to permeate the entire city. Every landmark looked familiar. I could almost remember the broad streets, squat buildings, and light brown hills. The city seemed eerie, haunted by the ghosts of forgotten success and anonymous failure.

Of course it seemed that way. The streets of L.A. are the real-life backdrops for the stories in the films and television shows I'd grown up watching. I'd seen the city before, but only in art, so its reality seemed strange and impossible.

I parked in the far lot and had to make my way to just under the water tower at Warner Bros. Studios, the same water tower my favorite characters had popped out of at the end of the Looney Tunes cartoons I'd watched as a child. I passed through security and began to navigate the labyrinth that is a major studio lot on my way to meet Alan for the recording session.

The Warner lot is an enormous campus of sound stages where major film and television projects are produced. Inside these airplane hangar–sized buildings are perfectly silent warehouses where any imaginable set can be erected. For exteriors, there's a "New York Street," two or three outdoor blocks that mimic a generic New York neighborhood. Many New York City scenes in films and TV shows are shot here—not in Manhattan, but in Burbank, California.

I walked past the sound stages and New York Street and found my way to the Eastwood Scoring Stage, the Warner recording studio. The building itself is large but unassuming in comparison to the massive scale of everything else on the lot.

Inside, the broad hallway is equipped with a ramp for heavy equipment like harps, timpani, and pianos. The ramp and the stairs next to it cover an elevation of only a few feet: the studio's live room rests on layers of wood and rubber to insulate it from the sounds of traffic that might carry through concrete.

I was escorted through a heavy wooden door that separated the studio from the rest of the building. The door was a sonic airlock, and as it closed behind me, it seemed to seal off outside sound. I walked past an office and through another equally large wooden door into the control room. It was buzzing with conversation, but every sound was sculpted and perfect—even the voices of the engineer and Pro Tools operator, who were involved in a discussion about take numbers. The room was designed as an ideal listening environment. Every flat surface was deliberately covered in hard material to reflect sound or padded material to absorb it. The wall treatments had been designed, built, and installed with mathematical precision in consultation with an acoustician.

Aesthetically, nothing in the room looked like soundproofing because it was all covered in warm, thin upholstery fabric surrounded by lightly lacquered hardwood molding. Those eggcrate wall panels you see in photos of recording studios are not soundproofing. They're sound diffusors, randomly scattering soundwaves so they don't collide with one another or echo. Actual soundproofing is in the walls.

What makes a room truly soundproof is not wall treatment, however, but mass and space. Professional recording studios are usually built as a room inside a room, with two sets of thick walls and a lot of space between the outer room and the inner room. The best studios make this sonic architecture invisible.

A ninety-six-channel mixing board stood in front of three speakers made of beautifully curved and polished plywood housing—the most high-fidelity sound speakers available. In front of the board and the monitors, a picture window–sized glass pane, part of a meticulously designed and constructed glass matrix, allowed a clear view into the live room while rejecting all sound in either direction.

Just behind the board, a large table held several computer stations, and lush, brown leather couches for guests were behind that. The overstuffed couches were not only comfortable; their mass trapped bass frequencies, so they were another part of the sound of the recording studio.

Every studio is a musical instrument, like a guitar or a piano, and has its own character. I borrow this insight from producer and philosopher Brian Eno, who popularized the concept. He was one of the instrument's first masters and has written extensively on the subject. I knew intellectually that a studio was an instrument, but I'd never truly felt it until that day, when I stood in one of the most finely tuned recording instruments in the world.

In 60,000 years, we've gone from the crude manipulation of breath through a bone flute to a purpose-built room the size of an airplane hangar where sounds from any source can be precisely captured, controlled, and manipulated.

In the minutes before the orchestra arrives, the control room and live room of a recording studio have the energy of a space shuttle launch. An incredibly complicated and sophisticated instrument is being turned on and readied for use by a team of skilled professionals. This process begins the night before the session, and all the technical preparation needs to be completed before a note is recorded.

In the control room, Alan warmly welcomed me and introduced me to the crew. Sitting at the console (also called the mixing board, or sometimes just "the desk") was Alan's orchestrator, Kevin Kliesch. Kevin's job was to ready Alan's demos for the orchestra. Alan writes a sketch of an orchestral cue, and Kevin fleshes out the skeleton by deciding which and how many instruments need to play each part and what specific articulations they should use. Each composer and orchestrator work together differently, but usually the composer is more like an architect who decides how a building will look and what it will feel like to walk around inside it; the orchestrator is closer to the person who decides how the building will be fabricated.

Both composer and orchestrator do what most people would think of as "composing." What makes a piece of music world-class is a mastery of detail. The orchestrator pays attention to different details than the composer. Even composers who do their own orchestration usually do it in a second pass once they've sketched out the ideas. Franz Schubert, for example, left numerous sketches of unorchestrated and unfinished work, indicating that his process was "sketch first, orchestrate later."

Every composer I know works this way, especially when writing for large ensembles.

To Alan's left was Frank Wolf, the engineer. If the recording studio is an instrument, the engineer is the musician who plays it. The choice of microphones, the placement of each mic, and how the sound from that mic is colored and routed through the mixing board are decisions made in advance by the engineer. For a session like this, dozens of microphones are used, and the engineer places and soundchecks every single one. This can take hours, even with the help of several assistants. If microphones are incorrectly positioned, the sound waves they record can hit the mics at the wrong parts of their amplitude and cancel each other out. Microphones for an orchestral session must be placed with absolute precision.

Next to the engineer sits the Pro Tools operator, usually another engineer or an engineer apprentice. The operator is responsible for recording the sounds coming from the mixing board. He's also responsible for editing and creating takes as the recording progresses. He is the only person on the front line using a computer. Everyone else sitting close to the board is just listening.

At the second desk, behind the Pro Tools operator, is the session producer. In this case, the producer was someone from Disney's music department who was primarily listening for the quality of the recording and serving as a technical backup for the engineer. He had also handled many of the session's non-musical logistics. For instance, he'd arranged my parking spot.

Next to the producer was the orchestra contractor, who hired all the musicians. As anyone who's ever tried to get seventy to a hundred people in the same place at the same time knows, it's no small task.

The orchestra for a film score is not like a symphony orchestra with set rehearsal and performance times. Film orchestras are made up of many of the same players, but they're essentially pickup groups. Every film score requires a slightly different ensemble. For *Tangled*, Alan opted for a full symphony orchestra, but sometimes scores call for a string quartet, a small orchestra, just strings, or a few strings and some woodwinds. Whatever the lineup, the contractor's job is to fill the chairs with the best musicians who are available and suited for the style of the score. In addition to the creative and logistical work, the contractor is responsible for the completion and timely submission of the onerous union paperwork. It's boring and detailed, but it's the basis for a complicated and highly remunerative system of royalties paid annually by the musician's union. For a player who regularly plays union sessions, this annual royalty payment can be in the six or seven figures.

Next to the contractor sits the music editor. Although I would later become one, at this point in my career, I had no idea what a music editor did. Even after *Tangled*'s music editor, Earl Ghaffari, patiently and clearly explained his role to me, I still didn't get it, because I didn't know enough about the way a large production worked to understand his explanation. In my small studio operation in New York, I did all these jobs, often simultaneously, because I didn't work on projects that could afford the specialization that is standard in professional recording.

The initial meeting between the director and the composer, which happens well in advance of the recording, is called a spotting session. At this session, the director shows the composer a work-in-progress cut of the film and decides where music will go and how it will sound. The music editor takes notes and turns them into a list of all the music cues in the film.

A film, any film, is a series of photographs called frames, displayed at a rate of approximately twenty-four per second, creating the illusion of motion. Each of the approximately 175,000 frames in a film gets a unique timecode number. The document the music editor develops, called the "spotting notes," is a single spreadsheet listing all the music in the film with start and stop times in timecode numbers. Each discrete piece of music in a score gets a name and a number on the spotting notes like "m1," "m2," "m3." The composer writes each of these pieces individually. Once he's composed all the music listed on the spotting notes, and once the director has approved the pieces, the score is ready to be orchestrated and recorded.

Inside the live room where the orchestra plays, another engineer is responsible for headphones. Every member of the orchestra wears headphones while the recording is in progress. Headphones are needed so the performers can hear the click track (which is like a digital metronome) and the prerecorded elements (like synthesizers, or soloists) without those sounds being caught by the microphones. The engineer responsible for the headphone mix has a separate mixing console inside the live room to manage this complicated balance.

The copyists also set up in the live room. Each of the sixty-five musicians in the orchestra has a customized part on letter-sized paper. The conductor, orchestrator, and composer have large-format scores in tabloid size, and everyone else in the booth follows along with a legal-sized score. All these scores and parts need to be printed, checked, collated, and bound together by a copyist. In an orchestral recording session, several copyists are needed just to prepare and handle all that paper.

Before this session, I'd never seen, or even conceived, of music being made with this level of attention to detail or with a team this large, skilled, and specialized. If I'd walked out of the studio before any music had been played, I might have already learned enough to move my career forward. At that point, I'd traveled the world, heard my music on the air, and won an Emmy Award, but in that studio, I realized I was a talented hobbyist, a prosumer.

Already, I understood why Alan couldn't give me much advice on the phone. Our knowledge gap was so wide that nothing he could have told me would have made sense. I needed to see his operation with my own eyes. Almost everything I saw at Warner that day was something I didn't know that I didn't know.

I'd been around music production my entire life. I'd worked as a production assistant and associate producer at the world's largest sporting events, like the Stanley Cup, the US Open, and the Olympics. I'd been in many of the best control rooms on

Earth. The feeling inside a control room run by highly skilled professionals is the same everywhere, characterized by a palpable, calm competence that comes from deep expertise and intense preparation. The atmosphere in the Warner control room that day went beyond calm. It was serene. With so much talent in the room, a fantastic result was inevitable, and everyone knew it.

Although he was at the helm of this complicated, expensive endeavor, Alan was relaxed, a master surrounded by masters. He was excited about the music, but he didn't use any energy worrying about technical details. It was the opposite of the way I felt during every session I'd ever organized. During my sessions, I was obsessed with the technical details because they often went awry, and my small team didn't know how to fix them. Technologically induced chaos and disorder reigned supreme, so dealing with the technology seemed like the most important job in the room. The music was almost an afterthought, and it felt like we were working for the technology, not the other way around. Seeing Alan and his team at work, I realized that if I wanted to master music, I'd have to reverse this paradigm, and the only way to do that was to master the technology so completely that I could control the chaos and make the technology seem invisible.

Alan or one of his trusted team members had mastered every technical detail. All he needed to do during the session was communicate with the directors and think musical thoughts. The people and technology in the room would realize and capture the sounds he'd imagined.

His team was prepared. They'd worked at this level for decades, and they were all world-class, from the copyists to the musicians to the engineer handling the headphone mix. By my rough estimate, the orchestra and the recording team had clocked a combined two thousand years of experience making music.

When I booked a non-union recording session in New York, I'd agree on an hourly rate with the musicians and hire them for however many hours I thought I'd need them. It was informal and imprecise. By contrast, a union recording session is booked in three-hour increments, with an optional hour of overtime available if the contractor has arranged it in advance. Each hour includes a ten-minute break, so, like a psychiatrist's, a musician's hour is only fifty minutes long. In a session like the one for *Tangled*, each one of those fifty minutes costs the production company about $300. At that rate, there's no room for error.

The musician's break time is sacred. If the session goes over by even a second, the musicians are entitled to overtime. Large digital clocks with hours, minutes, and seconds are placed in both the live room and control room. Usually, the musicians would rather finish a take even if it means a few extra seconds into the break, but technically, if they stopped playing when that clock hit fifty minutes past the hour, they'd be within their rights, even if they were in the middle of a phrase.

The start of the session is known as the "downbeat." For the *Tangled* session, the orchestra began to arrive about thirty minutes before that. Technically, the musicians' call time is "be in your chair with your instrument in your hand and ready to play at exactly the downbeat," but these were all seasoned professionals, so they arrived early enough to settle in.

At exactly 10:00, the orchestra was seated, and the conductor was at the podium. Alan walked into the live room to give his customary short speech and thank the orchestra and crew for their hard work.

At 10:01, everyone was in their place. I was sitting on the couch in the back of the control room with a score in my hand. Alan pressed a button to speak into the conductor's headphones and said, "Let's start with m1. It has a lot of the thematic material we'll use this hour, so we'll all get familiar."

The conductor nodded, and said confidently to the orchestra, "M1 please, m1." Papers rustled, and in about three seconds, the entire orchestra was silent and looking at the conductor.

"Eight free to bar one," the Pro Tools operator said. This meant the orchestra would hear eight beats of a click track to indicate the tempo before they began playing the piece at bar one. The operator pressed "play," and a cinema-sized screen lit up behind the musicians, projecting the film without sound. The orchestra began to play the complicated, intense music as if they'd been rehearsing it for weeks, but they were all sight-reading—seeing it for the very first time.

The film playing behind them was strange. The animation was mostly finished, but all the characters had hair that didn't move with their heads, or they were just bald. I learned later that hair takes a long time to animate and render, so it wasn't completed, but since it wouldn't affect the placement of music, they left it out of the composer's cut.

The cue m1 was about two minutes long. It sounded huge, amazing. It was a little darker than I would have expected from Alan, which made it even more interesting. It had extremely complicated passages, extended techniques, and unique sounds, but it was also lyrical and funny in all the right places.

The composition was gorgeous, and the musicians had sight-read it perfectly, played their solos with delicacy, added urgency to the driving ensemble sections, and executed the most challenging passages with precision—almost perfection. It sounded as crystal-clear as it would if we had been in the room with them, but we were in a soundproof space, listening to the engineer's brilliant skill through speakers.

When the cue was over, I stood up almost involuntarily and stopped myself just short of applause. The virtuosity I'd heard was so deep, no other response was possible. Everyone heard me stand up, and all eyes were on me. I was supposed to be a fly on the wall, so drawing attention to myself was bad. The last thing I wanted to do was a waste even a second.

Alan chuckled. "It's Lucas's first session." The tension in the room broke and all eyes turned back to Alan. "That was great," he told the conductor through his headphones. "Let's get the violas to do more of an accent on the downbeat at measure 41, and the violins should touch measure 50 with those harmonics. Really nice read, guys."

The conductor made notes. The orchestrator asked the

timpanist to switch to harder mallets and gave the woodwinds some instructions. The conductor translated this already efficient language into about eight words. Then, the producer told the engineer, "There was a stage noise at measure 32."

"Playing back," the Pro Tools operator said. He played the previous take starting at measure 30, and at measure 32, there was the faintest sound of a cello bow grazing a piece of paper.

"Man, good catch. A mouse fart wouldn't get past you," said the engineer. This was a high compliment. In musical parlance, a great engineer can hear mouse farts, and a great sight-reader can read fly shit.... Don't ask me why.

The take I'd heard and almost applauded for wasn't good enough to be considered for the master recording. Before that moment, I'd never imagined how much I had to learn to compose music for an orchestra. Alan's name was on the score, but a hundred people were making music in the studio that day. I needed to learn what they each did and to take into account musical considerations I never knew existed. Everyone in the room was so comfortable with the advanced technology that it was never discussed, and that struck me hardest. Thanks to the unseen, meticulous preparation and maintenance of the studio's tech team, it ran perfectly, and everyone in the room knew its capabilities and limitations.

In the instant before the Pro Tools operator announced "Take two," I decided to move to Los Angeles and apprentice with a film composer. Six months later, I drove across the country in my fifteen-year-old Toyota to begin my career as a composer.

REMOTE CONTROL

My first week in Los Angeles began with an interview at Hans Zimmer's Remote Control Productions and ended with me covered in blood somewhere in California's Antelope Valley.

Remote Control Productions was run like a pirate ship: four buildings filled with composers who worked independently and sometimes with, or for, Hans. Their roles changed to fit the needs of the many projects he was either supervising or composing. A constant churn of roles and responsibilities, all lucrative and with the possibility of bestowing lasting wealth and fame on anyone who distinguished themselves, made Remote Control an incredibly high-energy, competitive environment, and Hans kept it that way.

An inhuman level of hard work was the norm, and sleep was frowned upon, so burnout was inevitable for all but the most dedicated, talented, and focused acolytes. This was implicit in every facet of the design of the production complex. The studios were windowless, devoid of natural light. Junk food was constantly available, because munching keeps you awake. A shower room was off the common dining area, and just outside it sat an oversized railroad clock without hands, because it didn't matter what time it was. Grab a handful of trail mix, take a shower if you need it, and get back to work.

What was the work?

The music for *The Lion King*, the Pirates of the Caribbean movies (all of them), the Transformers movies (most of them), all three Christopher Nolan Batman movies, *Inception*, *Interstellar*,

Game of Thrones, both of Denis Villeneuve's Dune movies, and *Man of Steel* were all written at Remote Control by Hans or one of the many composers who worked alongside him. The list of projects is several pages long, but you get the idea.

While I was living in New York, I'd heard about Hans's production complex and asked around about how to get a job there. A friend knew one of Hans's top composers, Michael A. Levine, and was able to set up a meeting for me.

Michael's studio at Remote Control Productions was an oddly shaped, windowless room lined with tatami mats and bamboo. It felt warm, inviting, and alive, a stark contrast to the sterile concrete hallways outside its soundproof double doors. The studio was furnished with a leather sofa and a live-edge cherry wood coffee table, too beautiful and finely finished for me to desecrate by placing my drink on it.

As if he sensed my hesitation, Michael casually put a sandstone coaster down as he filled my cup with coffee. The blue glow of six computer screens backlit his stylishly shaved head as he sat in his Herman Miller desk chair, and I perched nervously on the edge of the plush leather sofa. My eyes wandered over the many different types of wood, each with its own distinct shine in the unnatural, sunless light.

Michael is most famous as the composer of the Kit Kat song generally known as "Gimme a Break." He'd gotten his start writing jingles in the 1980s and '90s: an incredibly lucrative, if largely anonymous, occupation. He'd also written a lot of concert music and was Hans's go-to composer for "out of the box" projects.

FROM MYTHS TO MICROCHIPS

Michael A. Levine and his studio at Remote Control Productions. COURTESY QUANTUM WEIRDNESS INC.

When I met him, he'd just finished scoring a show called *Cold Case* for CBS, which ran for seven seasons and was in syndication, so he was looking for his next project. We were the same kind of friendly and hit it off instantly, bonding over a shared love of jazz and literature. I think he enjoyed my snarkiness and New York severity, which the Southern California sunshine hadn't yet bleached out of me.

In New York, I worked in a studio with an analog recording console. The computer basically performed the function of a tape machine. The sounds came from the instruments we recorded, the mics we used, and the circuits in our analog board. The session I'd seen at Warner Bros. worked the same way: the gear was there to capture and color sound, not to generate it.

Michael's studio at Remote Control was capable of recording analog sounds, too, but its primary function was to make orchestral music digitally. Between his tatami-matted room and his assistant's comparatively spartan office, nine networked computers were housed in a short, wide, air-conditioned hallway. It was called the "machine room," and it was the heart of the studio. All the monitors and keyboards at the various workstations were terminals for computers mounted on the nineteen-inch-wide racks in the machine room. At the time, it was cutting-edge music technology.

After a long, engaging chat, I told Michael I was in Los Angeles to learn about his job and how to use computers to make music. I told him I had no idea how his gear worked and wanted to apprentice myself to someone so I could learn. He offered me an unpaid internship, and I enthusiastically agreed to help in any way possible for a few days a week. We met on a Wednesday, and I was to start the following Monday.

That weekend, I decided to celebrate by taking a trip. It would be my last chance for at least a few months to explore my new city. In the few minutes I'd spent at Remote Control, I'd sensed that working there, even as an intern, would be all-consuming.

My girlfriend and I decided to drive north and cut through Canyon Country. Our wandering led us through landscapes and past public works projects whose scale seemed impossible to our Northeastern imaginations. We traversed a mountain pass, saw some enormous waterworks, and drove through desolate, otherworldly rock formations and past endless, dusty farmland, arriving at Lancaster, California.

It's called a city, but it's really more of a town on the outskirts of the almost unimaginably large County of Los Angeles. We had lunch at a trendy bowling alley where the scoreboards were touchscreens and everything looked simultaneously retro and brand-new. We bowled a few frames and decided to head home.

I suggested that she drive. She had a license, but as a lifelong resident of New York City, she'd only driven during vacations. If she was going to survive L.A., she'd need to practice. As we sped down the straight, vast highway, something startled her; I still don't know what. She jerked the wheel to the right, and we barreled toward a canyon wall. I felt almost like the impending horror was happening on a TV screen, and I was just a spectator—until the front end of the car slammed into the rocks.

The initial impact cracked the windshield, and the vehicle's interior filled with smoke from the airbags. The car bounced off the slope of the canyon wall at seventy-five miles per hour, flipped over, and slid for about three hundred yards.

Some people say accidents like this seem to happen in slow motion, but my experience was excruciatingly fast. I had just enough time to understand my situation and know that no reaction was possible. All I could do was hope to emerge alive.

As the car slid down the highway on its roof, my mind was

able to distill all the fear, adrenaline and emotion into a single, silent articulation: "If we hit a solid object, we're dead."

By the time I'd formed this thought, we'd stopped, upside down and strapped into our seats. My girlfriend was shaken but totally unharmed. I had cut my forehead on something and was bleeding profusely, although the wound wasn't deep. I was in shock, so I didn't know that I'd also fractured my back at the L2 vertebrae. The blood was more dramatic, but the fracture was serious. We managed to get out of the car, and I lay down on the side of the road, bloody and disoriented. A passerby must have called 911; an ambulance arrived, and I was rushed to the nearest hospital, immobilized and strapped to a stiff board to prevent further injury.

I was in no condition to begin my internship that Monday. I spent the next few days in an opioid stupor, seeing doctors, buying a new car, and adjusting to my diminished physical capacity.

Twelve years later, I haven't fully recovered, and while I avoided addiction, I definitely learned how seductive opioid pain medications can be. I can't touch them ever again. If I'm not diligent with physical therapy, diet, and exercise, my back still seizes up and sends shooting pain down my leg.

Despite my injury, I managed to begin my internship a few days later. I was in a new city where I had few friends, unable to do much of anything but sit in a chair learning my craft. By the twisted logic of an artist obsessed with mastery, it was a perfect situation.

Creating music with computers is complicated, and it's

easy to become obsessed with the machines and forget what they're there to do. Music technology is so intricate today, most composers have at least one person on staff whose job is simply to manage the machines. Composers want the machines to be as invisible as possible during the composition process, in the same way that word processing software should seem invisible while you're writing. But, as I learned at Alan's session, making complex technology truly invisible is expensive and requires teams of dedicated humans. In the absence of specialized professionals, we get used to working with imperfect technologies so long as that saves more time than it costs.

That's a fine solution for something like writing words, where the technology is streamlined and easy to operate. But at the time I was at Remote Control, professional music technology was neither of those things. The nine networked computers in Michael's studio were part of a bespoke computer system designed for composing music. Eight of the nine computers hosted virtual instruments. The ninth one hosted a digital audio workstation (DAW), a program used to compose music. A DAW is to creating music what a word processor is to writing literature, allowing a single person to create something from inception to publication. Using a DAW, virtual instruments, and an internet connection, a musician can write, record, mix, master, and release a fully realized piece of music.

Because of this technology, contemporary composers can have every sound that has ever been used to make music at their fingertips. We're always looking for new sounds, always on the hunt for anything we can bang on, scrape, pluck, or blow—anything that adds a unique character to our compositions. By creating and purchasing virtual instruments, we can collect and store vast libraries of sounds. I currently have about twelve terabytes of samples, and my collection is mid-sized. It would take 2,200 years to play each sound in my library. While I use some of them every day, I'll never hear all of them.

Every sound that can be produced by a violin, viola, cello, oboe, clarinet, bassoon, guitar, urdu, oud, daduk, taiko drum... has been captured digitally, organized, and deployed as a virtual instrument available for free or for purchase. Any instrument you can imagine, and more you've never heard of, are a few clicks away from being usable in a digital audio workstation.

Because they're digital, samples offer infinite sonic choice but little opportunity to infer relationships between sounds and the physical objects that create them. I experience a visceral connection when I hear a master play an instrument, and I experience a similar connection when I play one myself. But when I use a virtual instrument, I feel no connection at all.

Some composers think the only way to master music is the old-fashioned way. Some think composers who use technology aren't real composers at all and only achieve the superficial appearance of mastery.

I think that's wrong, but if you haven't mastered the technology, it's easy to draw that conclusion. Strangely, it's even easier for some composers to draw the conclusion that their skills can be replaced by AI if they *have* mastered the technology.

FROM MYTHS TO MICROCHIPS

Just fifty years ago, virtual instruments on a digital audio workstation would have seemed like an unimaginable power, and the ability to use and manipulate any sound and create new ones without relying on musicians, recording studios, or even your imagination was inconceivable. It would have been obvious to composers that virtual instruments and digital audio workstations would make skills essential to mastering the craft irrelevant: things like an intimate knowledge of transposition, on-the-fly math to relate musical tempo to events happening on the screen, and the ability to create an eight-line sketch and orchestrate it. Today, a digital audio workstation makes these disciplines as important to composing music as good penmanship is to writing words: nice to have, previously essential, but no longer necessary.

Virtual instruments give the composer the power to hear, not just imagine, how something will sound. They shift the focus from paper notation to specialized graphics on a screen and remove a layer of abstraction between notated sound and actual sound. You can hear the sounds you notate in a DAW—not just in your head, but with your ears. This is such a radical change in the way that music is conceived and composed, its long-term implications are still unclear. Optimists think it will usher in a bright new future. Pessimists think it's a step down the road of music becoming a lost art, taken over by powerful computers.

Virtual instruments often comprise very large files, and opening a large file on a computer is time-consuming. It can take a few seconds to a few minutes to load a virtual instrument, and that small delay can break the illusion that the rig is an instrument, effortlessly responding to the composer's input, and interrupt the creative flow.

It's easy to brush this off and say that loading a virtual instrument might take fifteen seconds while arranging for a musician to play something would take at least a few hours. But in the throes of creative endeavor, time works differently. Time lost in the creative process does not have the same value as time lost doing administrative tasks. When engaged in any kind of creativity, interruptions are like an open door and ideas are like a skittish kitten who'll bolt out of the room at the slightest provocation.

Psychologist Michael Posner's studies of creative people at work have shown that it can take as much as twenty minutes to get back into the flow of creative work after even a minor interruption, like an email notification. While virtual instrument technology reduces a task that took a few hours to a few seconds, those few-second interruptions are a problem. Useful technology saves work, but it can only be a net benefit in creative endeavors if it saves the right work from the right processes at the right time.

A composer working with manuscript paper and a pencil is limited only by their imagination. A composer working with a DAW is restricted to the samples they have loaded and are ready to play. In 2013, a computer could only load about fifty virtual instruments at one time, but a composer might need hundreds for any given project. Hans Zimmer used the available technology to solve the problem of access to several hundred virtual instruments, making the creation of orchestral music digitally a viable option. It also made him one of the most successful composers in the world.

Before we get into his solution, though, let me tell you about a forgotten myth, a story about a king and a god.

In Plato's *Phaedrus*, he has Socrates share the legend of how writing was first given to the Egyptians by Theuth, the god of technology. In this telling, Theuth addressed Thamus, the wise king of Egypt: "Oh, King, here is something that, once learned, will make Egyptians wiser and improve their memories. I have discovered the technology of writing."

Thamus replied by telling Theuth that "one man can give birth to the elements of an art, but only another can judge how they can benefit or harm those who will use them. And now, since you are the father of writing, your affection for it has made you describe its effects as the opposite of what they really are. In fact, it will introduce forgetfulness into the soul of those who learn it: they will not practice their memory because they will put their trust in writing, which is external and depends on signs that belong to others, instead of trying to remember from the inside, completely on their own. You have not discovered a potion for remembering, but a potion for reminding; you provide your students with the appearance of wisdom, not with its reality."

Theuth always charged a price for his inventions. Perhaps trading memory for writing seemed like a profound loss to a pre-literate king, but the technology of writing is one of the foundations of civilization and its benefits were worth the loss of memory. Memorizing is heavy cognitive work, while writing is more durable and less costly.

King Thamus's response suggests that people who don't learn the old-fashioned way—in this case through memorization—can never achieve wisdom and will only achieve the appearance of wisdom. It's tempting to believe him, especially if you've ever learned something "the old-fashioned way," but it's not a very good argument.

Wisdom comes with experience, and experience comes with age. It hardly needs to be said that those who learned the old-fashioned way are usually old. They are likely to be wiser than those schooled in whatever the new way is, not by virtue of their education but by their long experience.

There's a tradeoff between new technology and time-tempered wisdom. With each technological advance, we must decide whether the wisdom it costs, if it costs any, is worth the benefits it bestows. This is difficult and sometimes impossible to calculate. Sometimes we can't predict what the effect of a new technology will be, so we use a shortcut, a subconscious calculation, to assess whether use of a given technology feels as though it saves more time than it costs.

Because I learned composition the old-fashioned way, it seems to me that those methods have useful, even necessary, benefits. Perhaps I don't want to face the fact that a significant part of my life was spent learning a skill I don't need. I'm disposed to think that new technology is slower and more cumbersome than working with paper and pencil.

Technology is doing some of the work I used to do, and at first glance, it feels like it will threaten my job as a composer, or even threaten all human creativity. If what I sell is the product, then anything that makes a similar product through a more efficient process is competition. But what I sell is the culmination of a process I've developed over half a lifetime, and it's unique to me.

Let's say that the product I sell is a recorded piece of music. What gives this product value is that it is the result of a chain of ideas I formed over a long period of time. The work composers do to get their ideas to market and the technology we use to do it have changed in every generation—sometimes slightly, sometimes fundamentally—for at least 60,000 years.

THE RIG

I met the musician and producer Quincy Jones, one of music's most revered figures before his death in 2024, at a party at the Hollywood Bowl after a concert of Alan Menken's music. Jones, who worked with nearly every notable person in the music business, from Frank Sinatra to Michael Jackson, was in a wheelchair, eating food he'd brought with him, attended to by two unbelievably beautiful women.

I knew that I'd only have a moment to talk to him. I let him know that I was a composer too, that I loved and respected his work, and that I'd appreciate any advice he could give me. Without skipping a beat, he said, "You have to master your recording technology; otherwise, you work for it and it don't work for you."

Jones had studied with the greatest classical composers of the twentieth century. He had hand-copied works by Ravel, reduced them to sketches, changed the key, and re-orchestrated them. He had used pencil and paper to write a big-band arrangement of Bert Howard's 1954 song "Fly Me to the Moon," which was famously performed by Frank Sinatra. He had mastered the trumpet and played with the greatest musicians in the world. He was eighty-six years old, but he didn't tell me to learn the old ways. He told me to master the new ones.

Hans Zimmer didn't learn the old-fashioned way. He invented a new way, an ingenious method to keep creativity flowing by networking several computers so that all the virtual instruments were loaded all of the time.

Hans, and everyone who worked for him, had what was effectively a private internet of sounds attached to their DAWs, called a "rig." This solution was expensive and complicated and forced composers to understand the details of computer networking. But these rigs were specific to the needs of each composer.

Each composer's rig is a unique musical instrument. The definition of a musical instrument—"an object or device for producing musical sounds"—doesn't even need to be stretched to include rigs. By telling me to master recording technology, Quincy Jones was advising me to master my instrument.

Every musician has to intimately understand the medium and available technology of the time. Gradually, since the time of the bone flute, Western music has atomized and specialized.

"Musician" used to mean "instrument maker, composer, and performer." Now, artisans create instruments for musicians to play, and music is written by a composer. This kind of specialization—an instrument maker who is not also the intended player of each instrument they make—is only possible in sophisticated, large-scale societies. An individual can carve a flute from a bone without taking too much time away from hunting and gathering, but a nomadic hunter-gatherer cannot make a piano.

The complexity of an instrument and the skills needed to manufacture it reveal a lot about the society into which the instrument was born. Flutes were portable and sounded good in the forest and on the steppes where our nomadic ancestors lived. The harp sounds good in angular, cavernous stone rooms, and specialized woodworkers are required to produce it; it came to prominence in Mesopotamia and Greece with the rise of cities and ziggurats, which were only possible thanks to agriculture and commerce. In the medieval period, when the church built scores of stone cathedrals and could support monks in their decades-long work of memorizing liturgical music, large male choirs became prominent. Choirs sound good in stone cathedrals and require a dedicated class of singers to maintain the repertoire through oral tradition. Flutes on a mountaintop, harps in a ziggurat, and choristers in cloisters.

Orchestral music required teams of instrument makers, musicians, dedicated buildings, and novel systems of abstraction like musical notation. Today, it also requires computer code and graphical user interfaces, and a single composer can use technology developed by thousands of people to produce music entirely by themselves, utilizing every instrument that has ever existed. We can work in total isolation to produce music without ever collaborating with another soul, but we usually don't. We use the technology to heighten and enrich our collaborations, and there are even technologies designed to connect one rig with another for the purpose of collaboration.

Like the flute, the rig is an appropriation of communications technology. What does it say about our society? As music gets more complicated, the people who collaborate to make it become further removed from one another, just as the instrument maker became distinct from the performer. It seems normal to me that I've never met the people who made most of my physical or virtual instruments.

I can imagine that in only a couple of generations, people won't think of virtual instruments as having been made, or of music as a collaborative endeavor with many humans in one place. Virtual instruments and music technology will become invisible elements of life, robust tools that composers will integrate to realize their ideas, in the same way that most professional musicians today don't think of musical notation as technology, or even as something that was deliberately invented.

To me, there's something magical and irreplaceable about a live concert. But maybe that's just a construct of our culture and my education. Maybe I'm not thinking outside the box. Maybe I learned the old-fashioned way and my views are too calcified to be molded to the realities of the near future.

FROM MYTHS TO MICROCHIPS

While it's disconcerting to imagine a not-too-distant future when music will be made on computers and never performed live, Western music has never been so close to the true roots of how and why it is made. Our tribe is bigger, our raw materials more complex, but we are the same musicians we've always been. A composer and their rig are the ultimate synthesis of technology and art. Although in the long term, some believe that this technology might pull apart the fabric of our humanity, in the short term, it makes creating and consuming music more accessible. For now, it saves more time than it costs. Our unconscious calculation, our knee-jerk reaction, can blind us to the obvious truth that the benefits of music technology are real and present, and its cost is just speculation.

Theuth's price, the cost of using a new technology to write things down, was sacrificing true mastery for convenience. But it's an outdated metaphor. Over time, technological progress, no matter how seemingly fast and catastrophic, is part of the nature of the art.

When I was at Remote Control Productions learning to use cutting-edge music technology, I didn't consider any of this. Working first as an intern and then as an assistant and music editor for Michael A. Levine, I was consumed by learning to play this new instrument. For the first few months, my only job, eighteen hours a day, seven days a week, was to learn about the rig.

Four of the computers used in Michael's rig ran on Microsoft Windows, and five on Mac OS. They were connected to six different monitor screens, six different speakers (which, confusingly, are also called monitors), and assorted other audio equipment. Cables ran through the floor from where the composer sat into the soundproofed and hyper-cooled machine room. The software connecting these nine computers ranged from professional-grade networking made and supported by Fortune 500 companies to an essential piece of software for sending music data over network cables made by one guy in a garage in the Midwest and used only by a few dozen professional composers. Sometimes, when I called him for tech support, I could hear what sounded like his family eating dinner in the background.

In addition to routine tasks like getting coffee and administrative busywork, I was responsible for keeping the rig running so that it was always available for Michael. I became the technical staffer who made the rig seem invisible to the composer. I'd never managed anything more complicated than my own email account, but now I was in charge of this intricate, finicky, bespoke internet of sounds and the servers on which it lived.

It broke all the time. Each time, I tried to get it back online as quickly as possible, but I'd have to track down the cause of the failure, which often took hours or even days. Now I can admit that in my first few months, I was often the cause of the failure, but even in the most capable hands, it was a delicate instrument.

There were many late nights and many sleepless ones. I slept on Michael's tatami mats, ate trail mix from the kitchen with the handless railroad clock for all three meals, and showered in that well-maintained shower room, although I lived only a few blocks away.

I'd sometimes work on a problem for hours and lose track of time. My room had no windows, so I'd leave the building in what I thought was the middle of the night only to find that the sun had been out for hours. I made a lot of stupid mistakes and learned many lessons the hard way. Eventually, though, I got to know the rig intimately. In a few months, I went from barely being able to fix a minor problem on my laptop to confidently using command lines on networked servers and taking computers apart for repairs. Simple stuff for professional programmers, but worlds away from my studies as a performance major in college.

The purpose of this incredibly complicated instrument, which cost about $100,000 and required a staff to maintain, was not even to create the final master recordings you hear in film scores, but to create realistic-sounding orchestral demo recordings. Was it really worth $100,000 just to make good demos?

As I mentioned earlier, an orchestra in a recording studio with all the required musical and technical professionals can cost about $300 per minute. In a three-hour session, a really good orchestra can record about twenty minutes of music. That means each minute of recorded music costs $2,700. Every film is different, but forty minutes of finished music in a film is about average. At those rates, recording the score to a film would cost

$108,000 on top of the composer's creative fee, which could be between $20,000 and $1,000,000 or more, depending on how famous the composer is.

Before composers had rigs, they made demo recordings with small ensembles or just a piano, which was time-consuming and expensive. Worse, the client—a director or producer—was usually not a professional musician practiced in imagining how the demo will sound with a full orchestra. They might pay the composer a six- or seven-figure fee in addition to the recording fees, but they'd have very little idea how the score would sound until they heard it in an expensive recording session. Many, if not most, great movies were made this way.

By creating the rig, Hans was able to make demo recordings that sounded almost like the finished score. Initially, they didn't sound great by today's standards, but they sounded good enough. He saw a problem no one else saw and knew that it had a technological solution. And he found a solution, but it was an imperfect one. As we've already learned from equal temperament and the problem of itinerant distance, imperfectly solved problems have unpredictable and wide-reaching consequences.

With his new technologically enabled process, Hans's clients could hear what their score would sound like before they paid orchestras to record them. They could sit beside him at his rig and watch him manipulate the music to fit their creative direction in real time. This $100,000 piece of equipment could help clients understand their substantial investment in his services, and it allowed them to comment on and make changes to a film score before it was recorded. It gave non-musical creatives involved in the film much more creative control of the score, and it gave directors access to the one area of filmmaking that had been opaque to them.

This innovation more than any other made Hans Zimmer the world's most successful composer. Today, most composers work like Hans, and clients expect the same level of control. Hans facilitated this further by ruling that specialized musical terminology was not to be used in meetings at Remote Control. He wanted his clients to feel they were in control, even if they didn't fully understand what they were controlling. I thought of Hans when I watched the Boston Dynamics CEO, Robert Playter, hand the remote control of a powerful and potentially deadly robot to his investor to let him viscerally experience what he was investing in.

It wasn't until I fully understood what Hans had done that I began to grasp the power of technology in the arts. With his incredibly expensive and complicated system of tenuously connected computers, he was able to do what any retail clerk or street vendor does to ensure a sale. He put the merchandise in the customer's hands.

Hans made it possible for non-musicians to meaningfully participate in the creation of music, a billion-dollar idea that revolutionized the process of composing music and made it a bit more user-friendly. More than anyone before him, Hans "democratized" the creation of music. The available technology was both the catalyst for his vision and the means of achieving it.

SAMPLING

What underlying technology makes all this possible? Sampling.

Producers of hip-hop and pop music use sampling to create a beat by looping short recordings taken from existing songs. Early DJs accomplished this by using two record players and a volume slider so they could switch the sound from one turntable to the other. They'd cue up two copies of the same record, play the desired four bars from one, then switch to the other while queueing the first one. The result was an endless loop of the same musical phrase. Today it seems simple, but in the 1970s and '80s, no one had heard anything like it—just the cool part of a song played over and over again. Technology made it possible to create a new sound using old sounds, and gave birth to hip-hop.

In the context of virtual instruments, sampling is a granular version of this practice. Instead of sampling a song, virtual instrument makers sample a single note at a time. They bring, say, a virtuoso violinist into a recording studio and have them play every single note and articulation on their instrument slowly and methodically over several days. It's a maddening, boring process.

Once the recording phase is complete, each of these tiny audio files is painstakingly edited and mapped to a piece of playback software called a sampler, which allows the composer to trigger each sound with a MIDI keyboard. The final product is a virtual instrument that can be played with an electronic keyboard and sounds almost like the original but behaves a bit differently.

FROM MYTHS TO MICROCHIPS

If the composer is making a demo to sell the idea of a film score, the difference is insignificant. But as rigs grew more sophisticated, and the public grew accustomed to digitally rendered orchestral music, composers began to sell the score itself. So, whatever we demo, even if we plan to make a recording performed by human instrumentalists later, the sample version has to sound good when it's played back with just the samples and no real instruments.

Today, clients are rarely willing to trust a composer to realize their vision without hearing it first. In many lower-budget film projects, even mainstream TV shows, the demo is used as the score, and no live recording takes place. Clients have learned that composers can make music sound good enough using samples, and they can save significant cost by forgoing a live recording.

The equipment needed to become a composer used to be a pencil, some staff paper, and about ten years of study. Today, it's several thousand dollars' worth of computer equipment, some technological know-how, and good musical ideas. Classical training is no longer necessary, and many of the most successful composers, including Hans Zimmer, are self-taught.

What does this new paradigm sound like?

The way samples sound informs what composers write. Because they're so expressive, rich, and detailed, woodwinds are difficult to sample. So, for most of the 2000s and 2010s, they were out of favor at Remote Control. Discrete, short sounds like a single piano key or drum hit make better samples, and for the past fifteen years or so, film scores, especially the lower-budget ones where the score is all samples, have favored orchestral melodies with *staccato* (short) note durations, beneath large percussion ensembles.

As non-musical creatives grew accustomed to samples, they began to prefer the sound of the samples more than that of an actual orchestra in some cases. As a result, composers have increasingly been asked to write music that specifically uses samples. Even when a recording session is in the budget, musicians are usually hired to replace the samples with their live performances—and the players are expected to sound like higher-fidelity versions of the samples they're replacing. I once had the odd experience of a recording session with percussion legend M. B. Gordy, where I had to ask him to record live replacements for samples for which his drumming was the original source. Musicians today, especially in lower- and mid-budget projects, are sometimes directed to sound like virtual instruments because that's the sound that clients have come to expect.

This is a bizarre effect, and to musical purists, it might seem like an unimaginable perversion, but it's consistent with the way music has evolved over human history. If we can get used to equal temperament music, which is audibly out of tune, we can certainly get used to the sound of a fake orchestra.

Music is shaped by the technology used to create it. The physical manifestation of music—the way it's performed, recorded, and delivered to the audience—has a larger effect on musical style than any other factor. The way music sounds in the real world has always been the result of the process used to create it. And that process has always involved some kind of technology.

One result of this is that new technologies enhance some modes of expression while restricting others. The plectrum banjo, a four-stringed instrument most readers will have never heard of, was the most popular instrument in the 1920s, but by the 1940s, it had fallen to novelty instrument status. A plectrum banjo is loud enough to be heard over an orchestra. A well-known soloist could draw a crowd, so the whole band got paid. This single feature, volume, made the instrument incredibly useful. But when instruments became amplified electrically, any instrumentalist could be a soloist. The plectrum banjo lost its technological edge and disappeared.

Imagine if, a hundred years from now, no one remembers the electric guitar. This idea is anathema to me as a guitar player, but that doesn't make it any less plausible.

Technology has also changed the human voice. Frank Sinatra's style of crooning popular songs softly and intimately only became possible with a microphone: without a mic, you'd have to belt to the back row even in quiet passages because you needed to be heard over the orchestra. This is why crooners became popular only when amplification became portable and affordable.

This effect is even present in the way we speak. The Mid-Atlantic accent, better known as the old-timey radio-announcer voice, accentuates the mid-range frequencies of speech while minimizing the highs and lows. These were the frequencies that were most audible on consumer radios in the 1930s and 1940s, but as audio broadcast quality improved, the Mid-Atlantic accent lost its utility.

This happens all the time. In music, this change is reflected in the way players approach their instruments. Entire generations learn to play the dominant technology of their time. Audiences and performers come to believe that their way of interacting with music is natural, since it's the only way they know. In every generation, audiences and musicians will see the technology they use replaced by newer technology.

If we're not careful, we'll all become grandparents who don't understand our kids' music and, like King Thamus, fall into the fallacious lament that the old ways were better. ("Music isn't what it used to be." "What are kids listening to these days?" "Music only sounds good on [insert the media of your youth here].") Those ways were undeniably different. Whether or not they were better is subjective. To those who, like me, spent years of their lives learning the old way, this idea is difficult to accept, but no less true.

As a media composer, I'm used to making demos. I've written some of the music I described above with short string textures and lots of percussion. I expect my clients will want to hear fully realized demos for every moment in a film score, so my final product should sound like a higher-resolution version of my demos.

Some, mostly those more silver-haired than I, might argue that these habits make me less of a composer than someone who writes music with a pencil and paper. But while the old ways are familiar, they're not always better. Theuth's price is often worth it. Some of the music I write would have been unthinkable to composers a hundred years ago, impossible to imagine. Like it or not, novelty is progress.

As I've gotten older, it's become increasingly tempting to talk about how things have changed. I want to believe that the years I spent learning European music theory and writing counterpoint exercises in endless notebooks were worth it. I want that belief to be validated by my peers, who learned the same way I did. But the evidence does not support this.

Hans Zimmer wasn't classically trained, but he spent as much time as anyone, and probably more, learning his craft, and what he couldn't learn, he invented. Part of the reason he doesn't allow musical jargon in meetings is that he remembers what it was like to be in a room full of musicians talking about music in an unfamiliar language. It's a barrier even to aspiring professionals, so Hans removed it for his clients.

At this very moment, a Hans Zimmer composition is playing somewhere in the world. He's generated billions of streams, millions of dollars, and his concerts sell out stadiums. If his music is missing something because he didn't learn "the old-fashioned way," audiences don't seem to mind. After all, the vagaries of any trade are opaque to outsiders. If the product of the tradesperson is consistent and available, it's easy to assume that the trade is simple. Most people don't realize that their favorite musicians, including Hans Zimmer, have a deep understanding of computers and digital music-making technology. Why would they?

Music is not an exercise in technical proficiency, a piece of technology to be mastered, or a problem to be solved. It's the byproduct of a rich intellectual ecosystem that takes several levels of abstraction for granted and requires mastery of many skills that are unrelated to the output of the system. It's a process, a mode of communication, and what it says is far more interesting to listeners than how it says it. The details are only relevant to professionals and the insatiably curious.

Some people believe that the "how" of writing music can be reverse-engineered from the "what"—that if a composer created something, and we can train an artificial intelligence on everything that composer ever wrote, the AI will have everything it needs to create that same piece of music. I thought this way for a long time. It seemed intuitive that the human mind worked just like the powerful computers I'd worked with.

I thought that the human mind was a programmable system—a "meat mechanism," as Thomas Edison memorably put it—and that music was just a set of rules that, when executed, could yield predictable results. I was right!

And I was totally wrong.

I learned how and why I was wrong when a Chinese mobile phone company asked me to finish Schubert's Unfinished Symphony using artificial intelligence.

11

Andante

BIG QUESTIONS

COMING ATTRACTIONS

Before we get to the Unfinished Symphony, let me tell you about the coming attractions.

If you've been to a movie theater, you've seen a theatrical trailer. Music for theatrical trailers is its own genre and composers have had extremely lucrative careers writing only this type of music. Usually, the music for a trailer is composed by someone other than the composer who scored the film. It's treated as a completely different project.

Trailers are not produced by movie studios but by advertising agencies with their own budgets and creative teams, managed by the studio's marketing department. A trailer track, as the music in a theatrical trailer is often called, can be licensed or commissioned for anything from $10,000 to $100,000 and up. About five hundred films are released every year, so music for theatrical trailers is a significant business.

Like all music, there's a formula for writing trailers—particularly for blockbuster movies—which are usually conceived in three acts:

Act One is sparse with lots of reverb, spacey sounds, and big percussion hits.

Act Two has more motion, probably a full orchestra, big hits an editor can cut to, and unique, jarring sound effects.

Act Three, also called "the back end," features driving rhythmic patterns in the percussion and strings building to a big, tense chord held for a few seconds before the title card comes up. Then the tension resolves, usually to a sustained bass note.

(During the back end, the edits are faster, and we see the hero, usually an actor we recognize, in a gloriously expensive costume surrounded by elaborately rendered, computer-generated sets.)

These commercials for films are extremely important to the movie industry. The typical film will budget almost as much on marketing as it does on production, or sometimes up to three times more. So, the budget for a blockbuster trailer can be as large as the total budget for a full-length independent feature.

Why do studios spend so much on theatrical trailers? Today, when media is mostly digital, a movie is an experience without a physical manifestation. The trailer is the studio's way to follow the strategies of Hans Zimmer, Robert Playter, and any retail clerk or street vendor. The trailer puts the merchandise in the customer's hands.

Audiences want to be surprised, but not too surprised. The

conventional narrative of a big-budget film finds a creative way for the good guy to win. In a Hollywood blockbuster, you're led to believe that the typical Hollywood ending is impossible. However, by a brilliantly conceived twist of fate or luck, the hero gets the girl and the bad guy is defeated.

Audiences expect a big Hollywood movie to go this way, and the trailer's job is to get them excited for the journey, let them glimpse the production values, and show them the stars who will guide them through this intense but ultimately safe story. The trailer is supposed to whip audiences into a frenzy and make them think that if they see only one movie, it should be this one. Nothing whips people into a frenzy like fast images and loud music.

Trailer music is unnaturally loud. A full symphony orchestra playing as loud as possible is just one of several layers of sound in a trailer track. There's also a layer of big, loud synthesizers, sometimes a rock band or EDM layer, and a layer of sound effects whose purpose is simply to make the whole production sound bigger. After all that, a layer of mastering is added to make the track seem even louder. Trailer music is unlike any sound you might encounter in the physical world. It's incredibly powerful—so powerful that most people don't even realize it's there, even though they've been exposed to hours of it. If you want to see the trailer formula in action, re-read this section just before you go to a movie theater. You'll see that most trailers follow this three-act structure and that most of the music is as formulaic as I described it. The formula exists because it works.

While most successful trailer composers work in the genre for years before they land a commission, I got lucky. The first trailer track I wrote was a huge hit. Over the Fourth of July weekend in 2013, Peter Shurkin, one of BMG's top executive music producers, called me on the recommendation of a mutual friend and asked if I'd ever written a trailer track. I said "No," and he told me frankly that I was the last composer on his list. He'd only called me because everyone else had gone on vacation for the long weekend.

He wasn't sure his bosses or clients would give me a shot, but he was out of options. It's not uncommon in the entertainment business to get a job simply because you're the only qualified person who's known to the producer and available. In this case, I was barely known to the producer, and I was certainly not qualified, but I was available.

I suggested that I could team up with Michael A. Levine, my boss at the time, whose experience and reputation were reassuring to the major-label client. Peter agreed and told me that the assignment was to create a dark and brooding cover of the Tears for Fears song "Everybody Wants to Rule the World." The cover would be performed by a singer from New Zealand who had recently signed with the record label.

Labels sign lots of singers, but few become superstars. Two of the three ingredients for success—hard work, talent, and luck—can get you a record contract, but you need all three to become a star. So, we didn't think too much about the singer beyond the fact that her demos were impressive.

BIG QUESTIONS

We went through endless revisions, rewriting the track more than twenty-one times. Peter was a very demanding producer who knew what he wanted and how to get it from us. We finally got the track to match Peter's taste, and he sent it on to the singer. When Michael and I heard her performance, we knew it was something special. She sang the part we wrote an octave lower than we'd intended, a range we didn't think was possible for a young female voice, but she made it sound eerie, confident, and evocative. Her voice had a depth and wisdom most singers don't find until middle age, if they find it at all. She was seventeen at the time. Michael, Peter, and I thought the song was amazing. She was a unique talent, and we were sure anyone who heard her would recognize its brilliance immediately.

The song was mixed and mastered, then sent to the film's marketing team for approval. We expected a fast and enthusiastic response, but we heard nothing. In my experience, if I hear "Yes," it's right away. The prolonged absence of "Yes" is how people in Hollywood say "No."

The marketing team chose another song instead.

In the world of advertising, a flippant rejection is way more common than landing the job, but it's always disappointing. The record company offered Michael and me a buyout agreement for $10,000. It was a rejected track with an unknown singer for a major label client I'd never worked with. I knew it was a bad deal, and I knew it was stupid to sign away any possible royalties beyond $10,000, but I needed the money and figured that goodwill with a major record label was more valuable than any song. Michael agreed with me, and we didn't even try to negotiate for a higher fee or a piece of the residuals. We signed all our rights away for $10,000 and split the money.

I wouldn't put the details of this deal here unless it had turned out to be an embarrassing and costly mistake.

A few months later, Lorde, the singer from New Zealand, won four Grammys, including Best Pop Solo Performance and Album of The Year. We were right to think her performance was special. She was hard-working, talented, and lucky all at the same time. And in a much smaller way, so was I. Because I'd produced a song with her, I briefly got to bask in the reflected glow of her success.

A big movie franchise, *The Hunger Games,* wanted to include one of her songs on their soundtrack, but they wanted it to be a world premiere. She was on tour, shrewdly extracting maximum value from her red-hot career. She had no time to go into the studio and make a track for the movie, but her record label had one track with her vocals ready for release, a song that had never been heard by the public: our cover of "Everybody Wants to Rule the World."

The film's marketing department loved the track so much, they asked Lorde to be the curator of the soundtrack album for the next Hunger Games movie. Her legions of fans had been clamoring for new music, and when *The Hunger Games: Catching Fire* soundtrack came out, the song was an instant hit. It was still a trailer track, shorter than a typical pop song with no real chorus. And it was structured in three acts, so the studio released an "extended version," which just repeated a few bars of the third act twice, but Lorde was a star and her star power made it a hit.

I've been asked many times to replicate my success with "Everybody Wants to Rule the World," but I can't. The arrangement Michael and I created was good, but without Lorde's voice it would be no more than a trailer track, a piece of music most people would barely notice. Its success was ten percent skill and ninety percent luck. We'd produced a decent cover, but it was a hit because it was performed by a star.

Composers have always been servants of the performers who bring their work to life. A piece of music is rarely, if ever, a self-evident work of genius. The audience usually comes to the theater, buys the album, or listens to the stream for the artists' performance. It's the artist, not the composer, producer, or songwriter with whom the audience develops a personal relationship, which is one of the reasons why music seems so intimate and emotional.

As with every success I've had in music, technology made "Everybody Wants to Rule the World" possible. Although we have a hit together, Lorde and I have never met. And I didn't meet Peter Shurkin, the producer from the label who hired me, until months later. I don't even know the engineer who tracked Lorde's vocals or where they were recorded. It could have been any studio. The entire project was done remotely in 2013, which was not at all unusual. I've never met many of my close collaborators in person.

All the work I've done for theatrical trailers and everything I've learned about them has come from people whom I primarily or exclusively know virtually. I've never been in a room with a trailer editor, never been physically present at a trailer recording session. I don't think I've even been paid with a physical check. The entire transaction and all the creativity happen digitally with collaborators from around the world, and the music is made on my rig. Composers, especially media composers, are quick to adopt new technology if it can help us work faster. Useful technology saves work.

After I learned to make music to fit a formula, and collaborated digitally with professionals around the globe, it seemed natural to me that an artificial intelligence could collect all my keystrokes and take the method one step further. Surely, an AI could learn how I was creative and become creative itself. I could teach an AI the trailer formula, right?

I was eager to learn about and utilize artificial intelligence in my work. Perhaps because I'd made an abrupt shift from analog to digital music-making when I moved to Los Angeles, I found the possibilities of advanced technology more fascinating than terrifying. I'd mastered both systems and felt the new digital tools were faster and more fluid.

I wrote earlier that colleagues who had always used technology to make music were more likely to believe they could be replaced by AI. I think composers who have spent more time with technological musical instruments, and who have thoroughly merged their creative process with the technology, tend to discount the decades of study and human intuition that go into their own music-making. Technology was there throughout their study, so they feel it's a necessary, intimate part of their learning. They forget that music is the whole process, not just the end product, and they give work-saving technology more credit for creativity than it deserves. Music technology is part of the process, just as learning to use a word processor is part of the process of writing a book.

I think this explains why many of my thoughtful, brilliant colleagues harbor an irrational fear of artificial intelligence and its role in music. They've misidentified the source of their brilliance and attribute it to the tools they use, when, in fact, technological tools only serve to enhance their own.

This is the same mistake I made when I thought that I would be able to make music as beautiful as Alan Menken's if I just had a bigger budget. I discounted the role of human experience and brilliance, and I had to see it in action to truly begin to understand it.

I had found new music technologies relatively easy to learn, and much less time-intensive and physically demanding than learning to play a traditional instrument. A rig can help me quickly realize a musical idea, but that's only useful if I have musical ideas in the first place and a vision of how I want to realize them.

So I wasn't afraid of technology, and I thought it could help me. In 2013, artificial general intelligence—the kind with human- or superhuman-level intellect, intuition, and creativity—seemed just around the corner. More than ten years later, computer science has rounded many corners, but AGI always seems to be just around the next one.

After years of using a network of computers, my rig, to compose music, using AI seemed like the next logical step. If some of my collaborators were people I'd never meet in person, why couldn't they just be computers?

I naively thought I'd at least be able to use artificial intelligence to offload some of the more mundane computer networking–related tasks associated with operating a rig. I could teach it to be a better composer's assistant than I'd been. AI wouldn't accidentally break the rig through its ignorance or get tired of doing repetitive tasks. I thought some kinds of formulaic music, like music for theatrical trailers, could be taught to an AI and generated at a human or superhuman level. The speed at which technology was growing made this idea seem intuitive, and not even particularly frightening. What would the world lose if some music for advertising was created by a machine instead of a human? No one has a bust of a trailer music composer on their piano.

MARBLE BUSTS

Marble busts—or at least plastic replicas—of Haydn, Mozart, Beethoven, and Schubert adorn pianos all over the world. Each of these composers revolutionized music and had a unique path to greatness.

Joseph Haydn spent his whole career working under the

patronage of one family—almost a day job. He didn't write any of his enduring work until he was well into his thirties. By the time his output began to make waves, a prodigy named Wolfgang Amadeus Mozart was already famous. From the age of four, he wrote and performed brilliant music effortlessly. Like Michael Jackson or Stevie Wonder, Mozart was famous all his life, and nearly everyone loved and respected his music.

Though not a famous prodigy like Mozart, Beethoven was recognized as a genius very early in his career. He famously lost his hearing in middle age but continued to write music. Most of his symphonic premieres were met with tepid reviews from critics, but all nine of his symphonies are now considered genre-defining masterpieces.

Schubert was a prodigy, but not a famous one, and what we now consider his best music wasn't performed in his lifetime. He only lived to be thirty-one, but before his death, he wrote nine (though some might say seven, or eight and a half) symphonies, fifty choral works, twenty piano sonatas, six hundred songs, and countless other works. He was a generalist, which set him apart from his near contemporaries. He viewed himself as a composer first and a practitioner of a particular musical form second. That made him the great-grandfather of contemporary composers, who must be fluent in many different styles and forms of music to create pieces that resonate with an increasingly musically literate public. He wrote more music in his eighteen active years than the venerable J. S. Bach wrote in his fifty-year career. Yet he would die believing he'd been a failed genius. His symphonies didn't become popular until several years after his death, when Felix Mendelssohn became music director of the Gewandhaus orchestra in Leipzig and revived them.

Schubert is most famous in contemporary popular culture for two things: the song we know as "Ave Maria" and his eighth, "unfinished" symphony. The phrase "unfinished symphony" conjures images of a lone genius slaving away on his magnum opus but tragically perishing before he can complete it. The truth is that Schubert probably failed to complete his last symphony because he misplaced the manuscript or just forgot about it. More than any other great composer, Schubert had a propensity to leave work incomplete. He composed in fits and often abandoned a piece. The strongest evidence that Schubert just forgot about his eighth symphony is that he completed a ninth one.

He sometimes wrote music on scraps of paper, such as discarded envelopes, and left them lying about, as though he needed to expel the music from his mind. Once he wrote it down, he didn't think much about its future. A friend of Schubert's once collected some of these scraps from around his piano and had them professionally printed. A few days later, the friend presented the work to Schubert, who played the pieces, said they were remarkable, and asked who the composer was. He had completely forgotten music he'd written just a few days earlier.

Haydn was born in 1732, and Schubert died in 1828. So, in just 96 years, Western classical music saw four of its greatest masters live and die in one city: Vienna.

BIG QUESTIONS

Eighteenth- and nineteenth-century Vienna had grand concert halls, the world's best musicians, and a wealthy aristocracy interested in supporting the arts. The Austrian emperors commissioned operas and symphonies. Even the lowest nobles on the aristocratic ladder could afford to hire a trio to entertain in their salons. Musical exploration was supported in the only way it can be, by creating paid opportunities for musicians.

Emperor Joseph II directly patronized Antonio Salieri, who would go on to teach Beethoven and Schubert. (Readers whose knowledge of this period is based on Milos Foreman's amazing film *Amadeus* should know that, in fact, Salieri may have envied Mozart, but he didn't kill him.) The emperor loved Salieri, but he also adored and supported Mozart. His rule drew great musicians to Vienna, and this concentration of great minds led to a musical revolution.

No one could have foreseen that in less than a century, music would evolve from the technical, liturgical style of the Baroque period to the harmonically dense emotionality of Schubert. But the Austrian emperor must have known that if he brought enough talent together, something revolutionary was bound to happen. Cognitive revolutions are ignited when great minds have the freedom to get lost in their work and communicate with one another freely.

More than a century after Schubert's death, during World War II, General Leslie Groves was tasked with building an atomic bomb. With the support of the US Government, he created a small city of scientists in the desert and set them to solve the many and varied problems that impeded the successful realization of this most devastating war machine. General Groves knew about the conditions that ignite cognitive revolutions, so to save Western civilization, he collected the best mathematical minds in the world in Los Alamos, New Mexico, and gave them the freedom to get lost in their work and freely communicate with each other.

To process the equations required to create the bomb, the scientists at Los Alamos built some of the first computers. These punch card–operated machines, which could do equations faster and more precisely than any human, were realizations of an idea proposed in a thought experiment by the British mathematician Alan Turing.

The concentration of the musical power in Vienna changed music forever, and the concentration of scientific power in Los Alamos changed science forever. When the world emerged from World War II with the power of computers, the stage was set to create the virtual world we live in today.

Schubert created the last symphonies of the golden era of classical music, and Turing invented the last machine necessary to connect the world forever. Both achievements were the culmination of decades of effort by thousands of people. Both were the products of teams of brilliant minds.

Schubert and Turing, geniuses though they were, stood on the shoulders of giants. And I stood on their shoulders when I combined the accomplishments of eighteenth-century Vienna and the United States and Great Britain of the twenty-first century to complete Schubert's Unfinished Symphony with artificial intelligence.

IS CONSCIOUSNESS COMPUTABLE?

"Our Technology Finished Schubert's Unfinished Symphony" is an irresistible headline for any tech company's marketing department. Why finish the work of a deceased composer? And why is the problem so interesting to technologists and the public? The very idea of the project, as I would learn while doing press around the premiere of the completed symphony, raises a lot of thought-provoking, even disturbing, questions.

If a computer can create something like a symphony, does that mean it can be creative? If a computer can be creative, does that mean it can think? And if a computer can think, does that mean it's conscious?

The idea that something as complicated as a symphony could be wrested from the mind of a deceased genius by analyzing his existing work implies that consciousness, or at least some important part of consciousness, can live forever through pattern recognition. This very odd idea seems intuitively true to me. It seems to be just outside of the bounds of the most advanced technology of our day.

If it is true, could other parts of our consciousness be decoded and immortalized? Are our minds simply "meat mechanisms?" Is consciousness just a part in the meat mechanism we call a mind?

If artificial intelligence can finish a symphony, maybe it

can also finish the work of scientists who died too young, or researchers who passed before their projects were complete. Maybe Einstein could be resurrected to continue his work in physics and move our understanding of the universe forward. What could humanity accomplish with an immortal Einstein who exists forever in his intellectual prime and has no need for food or sleep? And if we can make one digital Einstein, why not make a billion of them?

The belief that human consciousness can be deciphered from artistic products and pattern recognition, then uploaded to a computer, follows logically from Pythagoras's belief that "everything is number." But is this belief scientific, or religious?

Many brilliant people, including cutting-edge computer scientists, believe that resurrecting consciousness through pattern recognition is only a few technological advances away. Similarly, some believe that consciousness is storable within a computer and someday we'll have conscious computers and disembodied minds.

A computer that has the ability to truly think the way we think, without the limitations of our physical bodies and faulty memories, seems like a step toward general intelligence. An AI that can make the beautiful music we believe only humans can make seems like it must be conscious on some level.

So, is consciousness computable?

Most people have a knee-jerk answer one way or another, and it's interesting to notice which way your knee jerks when you think about this. To understand the past, present, and future of artificial intelligence, it's helpful to bear this question in mind and ponder it often. To use a flawed metaphor, make this question part of the firmware of your own consciousness.

Like all projects in which artificial intelligence defeats a human at a game or creates a piece of art, the headline "Schubert's Unfinished Symphony Is Finished by AI" suggests that consciousness is, in fact, computable, and assumes that position as fact.

But the declaration in a headline that "AI Has [fill in the blank]" is not a scientific hypothesis or a pronouncement by the academy that computer cognition has reached a new level. Nor does it mean that the artificial intelligence has "understood" anything. When you see "AI Has [fill in the blank]," you should read it as "Some Aspect of [fill in the blank] Is Computable." It's a much less interesting headline, but it's closer to the truth.

Some very smart people—like Thomas Edison—believed that our minds are no more than collections of electrical impulses. Like Plato and Pythagoras, Edison understood life's deepest mysteries in terms of the most advanced technology of his day. If you accept his premise, it follows that once these impulses are decoded by a computer, which is also only a collection of electrical impulses, the computer will possess our consciousness and be able to recreate it. But the belief that the essence of our thoughts, personalities, and ideas can be reduced to the firing of neurons is just a metaphor masquerading as a fact. It's another example of bending reality to fit the concepts we use to describe it.

And it's the latest in a long line of metaphors for consciousness, beginning with the philosopher Epicurus, who thought that the mind was a valley and each tree, bush, and rock represented a thought. Plato used the metaphor of an imperfectly struck coin to describe the body, but he also believed that the mind was a chariot pulled by two horses, one good and one evil, and that the charioteer had to steer away from evil and toward good. During the industrial revolution, philosophers likened the mind to complex, steam-powered machinery. We still use this metaphor when we talk about the gears in our minds turning or anger causing steam to come out of our ears.

In the early twentieth century, the mind was conceived as a very complicated telephone switchboard where the operator could connect thoughts. Today, it's common to use terms like "RAM," "hard drive," and "bandwidth." These linguistic tools are used to describe one's mental state and efficiently communicate a complicated mix of feelings and situations. When a colleague tells you they don't have the bandwidth for a specific problem, there is no physical issue with the information flow into their brain. They're saying they're overwhelmed in a specific, emotionally significant way and don't want to pay attention to another issue at that moment. But when a computer is "overwhelmed," it's a physical limitation. Too many of its silicon transistors are in use and not enough are left to be allocated to a new task. A rearrangement of priorities will fix the issue, and the computer won't feel stress, or regret, or guilt at switching from one task to another.

If our minds are computers, who's using them? All these mechanical metaphors incorporate variations of the homunculus, the theory of consciousness that posits a "little man," little charioteer, or little phone operator running your mind. They're complicated expressions of the idea that inside your mind, another mind is doing the "understanding." Viewed this way, it becomes clear that these metaphors say nothing about the nature of consciousness but merely shift the mystery of your mind onto the mind of the little man inside your head.

For our story, the important thing is that any pronouncement that "the mind is a [fill in the blank]" is just a metaphor, not a scientific fact. The nature of consciousness is one of the most philosophically perplexing questions in human history, and resolving it is well beyond the scope of this book. Experts know a lot about *what* the mind does. Brilliant people have spent productive lifetimes exploring the topic, but we know very little about *how* and *why* the mind does what it does. Any simple explanation would be incomplete to the point of meaninglessness, while a more detailed explanation might be so complicated it would be decipherable only to those fluent in the concepts and jargon of neuroscience. This is frustrating, but a common aphorism in neuroscience explains the situation perfectly. It goes something like this: If our minds were so simple that we could understand them, we'd be too stupid to understand them.

We don't know what makes our consciousness tick, but we do know that for a computer, electrical impulses on bits of silicon are the base level of reality. An artificial intelligence, reduced to its simplest form, is just a series of microscopic pieces of silicon that either do or do not contain a charge. There is no deeper interaction in a computer than that.

In the human brain, the correlate to those pieces of silicon is the vast system of electrical and chemical interactions that that is necessary for consciousness. But that system is not the same as the actual, first-person experience of consciousness. Brains are not uniform sizes or shapes, and we can't simply share our brain state with another person as though it were software and have them also share our thoughts.

The philosopher Heraclitus said, "You can't step in the same river twice." In the same way, it's also true that you can't have the same thought twice. By contrast, a computer can put itself in the same state an infinite number of times. It can even put another computer in an identical state.

A single digit on a single microchip may be too simple to yield complex behavior, but a computer is made up of so many of these simple machines, it becomes complex in the same way that many molecules can make a cell and many cells can make a living human body. Somewhere in that journey from molecule to man, consciousness emerges.

The idea behind neural networks—the architecture that powers today's machine-learning AI—is that if a single computer is analogous to a neuron, a large network of them should be analogous to a brain. Many connections might combine in new and unexpected ways and develop emergent properties like consciousness, intuition, and creativity. If nature can create man from molecules, surely man can create sentience from silicon, right? (The alliteration alone makes this seem self-evidently true!)

We don't know what a mind is or what the preconditions for creating one are. The best artificial intelligence can offer is the possibility that maybe, by tinkering with computers, we'll discover the preconditions for consciousness by accident.

Maybe, like most problems in the physical domain, applying more power will yield better results. Or maybe, once we give enough computers enough power and enough information, a form of consciousness identical to ours will emerge—or even a form of consciousness different from but preferable to ours. It's also possible that more computing power isn't a path to creating a mind. Machine consciousness, artificial general intelligence, and the Singularity may forever be just around the next corner. Today, anyone who claims that consciousness is computable is basically guessing. They're using a kind of reasoning that, ironically, is one of the hurdles machines are still unable to navigate on the way to consciousness.

In her excellent book *God, Human, Animal, Machine*, the philosopher Meghan O'Gieblyn points out that the pronouncements of today's AI evangelists claiming that human-level AI and brain uploading will soon be a reality are similar in tone and substance to the writings of tenth-century church fathers who rhapsodized about the immediacy of the rapture, the return of Jesus, and immortality. Their descendants are still waiting for Jesus, and our technological route to immortality is not much more promising.

No matter how impossible the idea of immortality might seem, "You must prepare to be immortalized" is a strong call to arms. It has rallied zealots since the time of Pythagoras and probably long before. But those who believed that they'd live forever in Pythagoras's cosmology are dead now. His followers, who immolated themselves to save him from a burning building, are dead. Pythagoras is dead, and even the beans he refused to disturb are dead. Schubert is dead, too, and you and I, dear reader, are not far behind him.

HOW TO PASS A TURING TEST

If you're among those who have witnessed the rapid progress of artificial intelligence with awe and a bit of fear and have concluded that there's no fundamental difference between the way a computer might think and the way the human thinks, you are in distinguished company.

Alan Turing, one of the smartest men who ever lived, thought consciousness was computable. Specifically, he thought a computer that appeared to be thinking would be indistinguishable from one that could actually think. This was a radical thought at the time. Consider the following quote from British neurologist Geoffrey Jefferson:

> Not until a machine can write a sonnet or compose a concerto because of thoughts and emotions felt, and not

BIG QUESTIONS

by the chance fall of symbols, could we agree that machine equals brain—that is, not only write it but know that it had written it. No mechanism could feel (and not merely artificially signal, an easy contrivance) pleasure at its successes, grief when its valves fuse, be warmed by flattery, be made miserable by its mistakes, be charmed by sex, be angry or depressed when it cannot get what it wants.

The above quotation is from a lecture given by Jefferson in 1949 when he won the prestigious Lister Medal. This lecture was delivered at the University of Manchester just after one of the first computers, the Manchester Mark 1, came online. Then, as now, technological progress stimulated academics and philosophers to ask questions about the nature and limitations of consciousness. At that time, it was considered a fact that consciousness was not computable. Until the Manchester Mark 1, there were no powerful computers, no machines that could do anything a clever human mind couldn't do.

The first time the Manchester Mark 1 was operated successfully, one reporter called it an "electronic brain," an innocuous cliché that ignited a firestorm of debate among academics. Of course, in postwar academia, a "firestorm" meant a few highly specialized British academics giving lectures and publishing papers criticizing each other's views in ways so subtle as to escape the notice of almost everyone else in the world.

Coded insults and subdued imprecations were casually tossed across intellectual battle lines until October of 1950, when Alan

Turing published his groundbreaking paper "Computing and Machine Intelligence" in the journal *Mind*, which settled the question of whether a machine could think. Sort of.

In the paper, Turing quotes Geoffrey Jefferson's Lister lecture and proceeds to say, "According to the most extreme form of this view, the only way by which one could be sure that a machine thinks is to be the machine and to feel oneself thinking. . . . Likewise, according to this view, the only way to know that a man thinks is to be that particular man. It is, in fact, the solipsist point of view."

Solipsism is the belief that the universe only exists in your mind, since you can't empirically verify anyone else's experience. It's just a thought experiment, but if solipsism is really the way the universe is ordered, I don't know why I worked so hard on this book, because you're the only one reading it, and I don't really exist. If solipsism is true, your mind is the only thing in the universe and all further inquiry is pointless.

Turing's paper proved, at least in principle, that there is no reason why a machine could not be said to think, even if the way it thinks is different from the way humans think. Notably, he focused not on the interior experience of consciousness but its external, observable aspects. He suggested that a machine that could convince a human observer it was thinking would be indistinguishable from a machine that could actually think.

To think, or even appear to think, is a high bar for a computer, but industries have been disrupted by far less capable technologies. The music industry—which was, after all, created by disruptive technology—has been remade several times over by ever more disruptive technologies. Despite, or because of, this, the industry continues to be among the most technophobic in the world. Every new technology is greeted with extreme skepticism until it initiates a hostile takeover and becomes the *new* music industry.

A clear example in recent memory is music streaming, which began as a nuisance record companies tried to sue out of existence. But in just ten years, streaming companies became so profitable that they took over the business and became the de facto delivery system for all music worldwide. While they began as adversaries, labels and publishers eventually had to make a deal with the streamers. Today you could be forgiven for believing that record companies invented streaming.

Despite the music business's institutional technophobia, musicians like me tend to embrace new technology. Every component of the rig I use to compose was, at one time, supposed to bring about the end of music as we know it. Now those technologies are essential tools for all professional musicians.

Solving complex problems used to be the exclusive purview of humans. We used to think certain kinds of reasoning were what made humans intelligent and conscious. Now, we're not so sure. While we still don't know what consciousness is, we know it's more than the ability to reason. Artificial intelligence can already perform inductive reasoning (deriving a general principle from available pieces of evidence) and deductive reasoning (starting from a general principle to reach a specific conclusion) faster than any human, and it will continue to get faster and faster.

I thought if I fed a music formula, like the one for trailer tracks, into an AI, the machine's deductive power would generate decent music, which could then be produced with realistic instrument sounds generated by a rig. In theory, since it would all happen on a computer, the combined technologies of an AI composer and a rig could replace a human composer.

For years, I was interested in working with a computer scientist to create an AI music program. I wanted to see if creating an AI composer was possible, and if it was, I wanted to be at the forefront of AI music in case my job as a human composer became obsolete. (As of this writing, I have not switched careers. My wife and I are both composers and are busier than ever, as are all our colleagues.)

In part, this is because the streaming services the music establishment tried to destroy have been unbelievably successful at driving up the public's viewing and listening time. More media is available, and people spend more time with it than ever. Artificial intelligence, the kind used to determine which show you might click on next, plays a large role in keeping people engaged and creates a bigger demand for content, which in turn creates a demand for the music I write. AI is helping me more than the savviest human marketers ever could. For composers today, the benefit of artificial intelligence is real and the cost is speculative.

Artificial intelligence uses deductive reasoning to sort you, the consumer, into a group, then uses inductive reasoning to generalize about your group based on the huge amounts of data it can collect about you through your interactions with the many platforms you frequent. It can sort you into a group with very specific parameters based on your behavior and make broad generalizations that will allow it to suggest content you're likely to want.

The problems with this approach are well-documented and obvious to anyone who uses platforms like YouTube, Facebook, Instagram, Netflix, Spotify, and so on. The algorithm, the artificial intelligence, serves you more of the content it knows you like, creating a questionably enriching but vaguely satisfying and addictive media environment. For all its powerful analytics, AI ends up serving you more of the same things you already consume, just as any human marketer would try to do. But even the hardest-working marketer can't produce personalized playlists and movie queues for millions of users at once.

The technology you carry around with you and wear collects more data about you than any human team of analysts ever could. In some cases, an AI can use this data to learn what you want before you know you want it, and serve you a mix of content designed specifically for you in way that was impossible when mass media was printed publications and scheduled television.

Sameness is satisfying, but novelty is fascinating. We had more opportunities to be fascinated when we were not delivered personally selected content. But being satisfied will keep people on the platform, and that's the goal, which is why YouTube most often recommends videos from creators you already follow and only occasionally suggests similar videos from different creators. The media you see is the media you vote for with your attention.

The algorithm has learned what movie studios already knew: people want to be surprised, but not too surprised. In many ways, a YouTube channel uses the same model as a scheduled TV show. Viewers gravitate toward hosts they like and learn about topics that interest them through the host's lens. The power of YouTube that linear television could never possess is in the granularity and accuracy of the user data it can collect—data that has made YouTube's parent company, Alphabet, one of the most valuable in history.

Decades ago, companies like Nielsen generated ratings for television shows by calling viewers on the phone and asking about their viewing habits. The problems with that approach are obvious. People lie or don't remember, and the human interrogators had to collect all that data manually, so the size of the database was limited. By contrast, Alphabet knows everything you watch on their platform, how long you watch it for, and where you are while you're watching it, and it knows almost everything else about you from your browsing habits, even if you browse in incognito mode.

When you engage with their content, it knows your location down to which room you're in, and it knows that what you're likely to watch on the toilet is different than what you're likely to watch in the living room. Alphabet tracks your movements, reads your emails, and listens to your conversations. Most people know this and either don't care or feel like the benefit of Alphabet's technology is worth the sacrifice of privacy. (Though if this is the first time you're hearing that Alphabet and many other companies invade your privacy in ways that would have been unthinkable a few decades ago, I'm sorry to be the bearer of bad news.)

With this glut of information, YouTube's algorithm can break viewers into very specific segments and serve them micro-tailored ads. You and another person can sit in a room and watch the same video at the same time on different devices and see completely different ads. Only a few decades ago, a human marketer couldn't have imagined this power, not in their wildest dreams. Powerful computers accomplish this by analyzing millions or billions of data points about you.

From YouTube's perspective, the creators are there to keep you engaged and on the platform between advertisements. The better the content, the longer you'll watch, so YouTube pays creators to make engaging content. From a purely mechanistic perspective, ad-supported media (which is just about all media) exists to fill time between commercials, drawing eyeballs to advertisements.

Artificial intelligence can keep you engaged and steer you to content you'll like without "understanding" anything about you or anything about the content you consume. It's a matter of inductive and deductive reasoning. Computers use metrics about you and match them to metrics about content, comparing one number with another. It's pure calculation, and it works.

When I create music, I use both inductive and deductive reasoning. It's a very important part of my job, but it's also the boring part. Peter Shurkin explained the trailer formula to me, but I could have used inductive reasoning to figure it out for myself. Theatrical trailers have a few things in common, so, having seen so many of them, I could have induced that they all follow the same formula, and if I applied that formula, my music would sound like a theatrical trailer.

I use deductive reasoning to compare my theatrical trailer music with other theatrical trailers I've heard to determine if I've made the right decisions about pacing and instrumentation. In theory, I could teach a computer to do both processes exponentially faster than I can do them and base its conclusions on more examples of music than I could hear in a lifetime.

This can be done, and it has been. That's what the technologist I collaborated with on Schubert's Unfinished Symphony did. Without human intervention, however, the result is consistently mediocre music in the best case, and total nonsense in the worst. It sounds like the music of a technically gifted student with no voice of their own, and no semblance of what I'd call "musicality."

What makes a piece of music desirable to a listener is the use of a third kind of reasoning: abductive. I use abductive reasoning when I decide that some of the many deductions and inductions I've made while writing music for a theatrical trailer are more important than others to the trailer's success.

Although they all use the same formula, trailer tracks can

BIG QUESTIONS

sound radically different, because each composer has their own "sonic signature," a term used by Susan Rogers and Ogi Ogas, in their book *This Is What It Sounds Like*, to describe the "you know it when you hear it" quality of musicians and producers. Each composer sounds like themselves, and their signature is developed over years of abductive reasoning about music. A composer's sonic signature is what their process sounds like.

You never know exactly what works about a piece of music, but you can make educated guesses. Listeners don't always know what makes them like a piece of music, either. Even if a listener can articulate what they like about it, they might not understand what they're actually responding to, or it might only apply to that one person in that one moment.

You can use induction and deduction to figure out how to make something sound like something else that has resonated with people in the past, but what will resonate in the future is an educated guess. This is why performers have good nights and bad nights. Sometimes you have a bad night because your technique is off; sometimes you nail the material and it just doesn't connect. How to create a piece of music that unfailingly resonates with the masses is still a mystery.

Making music that moves people, music they want to listen to and are willing to pay for, requires abductive reasoning, and artificial intelligence has trouble with that. It's not good at intuitive, educated guessing, especially over long periods of time, and that's a key component in creating music. Induction and deduction are important tools in any composer's toolbox, but abduction is just as important, and it's a missing ingredient in AI-generated music, maybe because it's so difficult to reverse-engineer an educated guess.

In his fantastic book *The Myth of Artificial Intelligence*, Erik J. Larson outlines in great detail the problems of abductive reasoning for a computer. Someone who claims with certainty that consciousness is computable by citing the many instances of computers that have accomplished superhuman feats of induction and deduction arrives at this conclusion through abduction.

Abductive reasoning is what makes artificial intelligence feel like it's always right around the next technological corner. We've come so far that an educated guess will tell you that consciousness, or a true electronic brain, must be a small step away. But an AI with any level of sophistication struggles to employ the faculty you used to make that guess.

There is very little serious, well-funded work on abduction. It's difficult, and it may be no more useful than existing tools in targeting ads or keeping eyeballs on platforms. In his 1950 paper, Alan Turing outlined the benchmark test to determine if a machine is truly thinking. An artificial intelligence could likely pass this test—which he called the Imitation Game and today is called the Turing Test—without the use of abduction.

Some experts believe that artificial intelligence has already passed the Turing Test. So why isn't your phone thinking deep thoughts, and why isn't AI controlling every movement of a Boston Dynamics Spot robot?

Turing used the Imitation Game to prove to himself that a

machine that appears to be thinking is indistinguishable from one that can truly think. A non-computer-related version of the game might work like this: One person plays interrogator, and two other people play contestants. The contestants sit behind a screen or in another room while the interrogator asks them questions and receives replies by handwritten notes. The goal of the interrogator is to figure out which of the unseen contestants is male and which is female based only on their written replies. The goal of the contestants is to fool the interrogator.

Turing proposed that a computer could be said to "think" if it could successfully fool an interrogator into believing that it is human when playing a variation of this game. There is a constant drumbeat of articles and papers claiming that one program or another has passed a Turing Test. The headline "[Some AI Model] Has Passed a Turing Test" is common, but the truth of these tests and their methods is always nuanced. The first computer program to pass a public Turing Test did so in 2014, and it was a bit controversial.

In 2008, when I was living in Brooklyn, I answered a Craigslist ad to participate in a Turing Test. At the time, I was a performing musician who knew nothing about computers, Turing, or artificial intelligence. I was always looking for new and interesting things, and at that time, artificial intelligence, even the narrow AI we take for granted today, was still science fiction.

I arrived at the apartment of Hugh Loebner, an eccentric New Yorker with wild grey hair and distinctive, pointy eyeglass frames who had endowed a monetary prize for any computer program that could successfully pass a Turing Test. AI research had shown little progress for decades, and serious researchers had all but abandoned the field. Computer scientists, whose research depends on grants and venture capital, refer to this period as the "AI Winter." AI wasn't showing promise in commercial applications and seemed to require datasets and processing speeds that didn't exist. So, this prize of several thousand dollars, which today would amount to a rounding error in a mid-tier AI company's Series A funding round, was substantial.

I was one of several human interrogators. Only one of the programs I interrogated using instant messaging for the five minutes I was allowed to interact with it came close to convincing me it was human. Before I realized I was being played, I thought Eugene Goostman, a Ukrainian teenager visiting New York for the first time, was a real person.

He began by apologizing for his bad English and explaining that he was a foreigner. I'd arrived at the test by responding to an ad, and I thought that maybe he had, too. I was always looking for new and interesting things to do; maybe this Ukrainian teenager and I were cut from the same cloth. When I asked him a question he couldn't answer or one he answered incorrectly, he'd change the subject, and I assumed this meant he didn't understand my English phrasing. The ruse fell apart quickly. But the strategy of changing my expectation of the conversation was a good one. The Loebner Prize was not claimed that day, but I think Eugene Goostman got the highest score.

BIG QUESTIONS

An improved version of Eugene Goostman fooled thirty percent of human interrogators at a Turing Test event in 2014, and the event's organizers declared that it had passed the Turing Test. Thirty percent is not a passing grade in any system I'm aware of... but according to Turing's criteria and the subjective judgement of one highly learned event organizer, computers have been able to think since 2014.

So why hasn't Eugene Goostman been deployed to replace humans at help desks and call centers worldwide? Why hasn't Eugene Goostman replicated himself, learned every fact in the universe, and enslaved the human race with an army of killer robots?

MAGIC TRICKS

I can turn a Mexican peso into a US quarter. All I need is a Kennedy half dollar and a peso, which I usually carry in my pocket. The half dollar is a bit bigger than the peso, so I'll show them both to you as I slide the peso behind the half dollar. Then I'll put the two coins in your hand and ask you to hold them tightly. You'll feel the two coins, one bigger than the other, and I'll ask you to hand me the bigger one. As you expect, it's the Kennedy half dollar, so what's left in your hand must be the peso.

I'll ask, "How amazing would it be if I could turn that peso into a quarter while you're holding it in your fist?" You'll agree that it would be amazing because it would be.

I'll say a few magic words and do some hand gestures, and

abracadabra: When you open your hand, you're not holding a peso anymore. You're holding a quarter.

I can really accomplish this effect, but you already know that it's not because I'm a sorcerer. You know it's a trick. If I were to perform it for you, my flourishing hand motions and flowery language would tell you that I was about to deceive you for fun, because these theatrical touches set parameters that are different from those of normal interactions. Unless you're a magician, how I accomplish this effect will be a mystery; but you won't believe I've actually changed a peso into a quarter, even though your senses told you that I did.

Eugene Goostman fooled thirty percent of the people who interviewed him, not with human-level intelligence, but with a similar kind of verbal misdirection and theatricality. Its programmers gave it a backstory that established abnormal parameters for conversation and redefined success in the context of the Turing Test. It was a clever trick, and its creators deserve a round of applause for fooling some very intelligent people.

But the clever bit of misdirection Eugene Goostman employed was created by humans. That ploy was no different from the hand flourishes and florid language I used to prepare you to be dazzled by a magic trick. It would be unethical, and maybe a bit silly, for me to try to pass off my practiced dexterity and unseen preparation as wizardry by doing the trick without those baroque touches. If I claimed to be able to do real magic, people would want to see real results. Actually changing pesos into quarters at scale could have commercial applications, but appearing to do so is no more than an amusement.

Since the beginning, many AI advances that initially appeared to be magic have proved to be just tricks: amusing, but not amazing. The Turing Test continues to be the benchmark for artificial intelligence, and, so far, no program has truly passed a rigorous version of it. Even the most sophisticated of the AI chat programs, which today are the Generative Pretrained Transformer (GPT) models, can't convincingly masquerade as human in a normal conversation for more than five minutes.

But can AI pass a *musical* Turing Test? It turns out that, in the right context, even super-fans can't tell the difference between music written by humans and by machines.

J. S. Bach, one of the most prolific composers in history, was born in present-day Germany in 1685. Today, 1,128 pieces of his music still survive. His influence on the trajectory of classical music was so strong that music historians date the end of the Baroque period with his death in 1750.

Bach wrote masses, symphonies, concerti, and many pieces for solo instruments that are still practiced by students and performed by professionals. I play a few minutes of Bach on mandolin or banjo each day as part of my practice routine. Bach never wrote for banjo or mandolin, but his music is so enduring, it's still used to build technique and virtuosity on almost every instrument. His compositions are as fundamental to Western music as Shakespeare's plays are to the English language.

Dr. Steve Larson of the University of Oregon was a brilliant musical mind and an expert in J. S. Bach's music. In 1997, he participated in a contest at a Bach festival where a pianist was given three pieces of music to be performed to an audience of aficionados. One was written by Dr. Larson, another was selected from Bach's actual body of work, and the third was written by a computer called EMI (pronounced "Emmy," it's an abbreviation for "Experiments in Musical Intelligence"). EMI and Dr. Larson were instructed to write pieces in the style of Bach.

After the pianist gave an emotive performance of all three compositions, the expert audience was asked which piece they thought was authentic Bach, which was written by Dr. Larson, and which was written by EMI. The audience concluded that Dr. Larson's piece was written by EMI and that EMI's piece was written by Bach himself.

I think this was a reasonably robust musical Turing Test, and EMI passed it. This test was performed decades before Google DeepMind or OpenAI. So why do human composers like me still exist?

Although EMI was invented by musician and technologist David Cope in 1981 and fooled an audience of Bach experts, it has not taken the musical world by storm. I don't think it has replaced a single human composer. In its forty-five-year lifespan, it hasn't made much of a splash at all outside electronic music circles where David Cope was a celebrity.

I think this is because its narrow application—creating music that is like other music—is interesting but not particularly useful: amusing, but not amazing. Since the invention of the bone flute, music has evolved with the technology that humans created, and it has evolved the most when that technology allows music to reach more listeners.

Jacob Ward, a correspondent on NBC's *Today Show*, would eventually interview me about my completion of the Unfinished Symphony and write a book about the way our technology is changing us. He maintains that "Artificial intelligence might do for everything what Google Maps has done for our sense of direction."

I think his observation has profound implications, but music is one thing and wayfinding is another. When planning a route across Los Angeles, my main considerations are efficiency and safety. Planning a route with a paper map is tedious and commuting is boring. (My car, like all cars, is equipped to distract me from the boredom of driving with music and other comforts.) Before Google Maps and GPS, if you had a good sense of direction, you wouldn't need to check your map so often, but it was only useful because we didn't have a more practical alternative.

Music creation, taken as a whole, is not a cognitive demand composers would rather do without. It's a joyful, stimulating, and deeply, humanly meaningful undertaking. While automating something like wayfinding may make our lives easier, automating music creation misses the entire point of this human endeavor.

There are two kinds of innovations in music. The first, technical innovation, makes commerce more efficient, providing a faster, easier way to get music to an audience or collect money for the copyright. The second, musical innovation, makes it possible to compose and perform new and different music.

Artificial intelligence has made and will continue to make technical innovations, but it will not replace human music makers. Instead, it will supercharge us and push us farther down the path of rapid innovation. Anything AI can do will become the baseline for musical creativity, and human composers will jump off from that point. EMI has been deployed as an amusing trick, but that's about all it's done in its career. Musicians know that EMI is no threat to human musicianship, so they're not afraid to push the boundaries of technological music-making. Their aim is to propel the art form further, not automate it out of existence.

FINISHING THE SYMPHONY

The music technologist, professor, digital instrument maker, and guitar player Mick Grierson looks, dresses, and talks like a professor, but he's a rock-and-roller at heart. His goal is to push sonic boundaries for human composers.

When we met in 2014, he pitched me on finishing Schubert's Eighth Symphony using artificial intelligence. I thought the idea was interesting, but it seemed time-intensive and totally academic. Artistic projects can sometimes take years to take shape and it would be five years before we would revisit the idea. I had another idea I thought would be more commercially viable: I wanted to use AI to create an automated production music library.

Library music is often used in commercials and sometimes

in theatrical trailers, sports, documentaries, reality television, and even feature films. When you watch a scene set in a bar or restaurant but can't quite make out what's playing in the background, it's usually library music. When you watch a commercial and the music is original but reminiscent of a popular song, it's library music. Library music is everywhere. Music libraries create a lot of music, offering a more affordable alternative to custom-composed music. A significant portion of their income is the royalties paid by performing rights societies like ASCAP.

Like trailer music, library music is formulaic. In the 1990s, when music libraries began to gain market share, the music sounded terrible. Sometimes background music shouldn't be interesting enough to distract from dialogue, so that terrible but inexpensive library music was used a lot, and the people who made it, even if they weren't great musicians, made a lot of money.

When I explained the business to Mick, he told me that AI could already make music more or less like the library music of the 1990s. So, yeah, why not automate and scale its success by creating an AI music library? If we combined Mick's AI expertise with my expertise in music and publishing, our automated production music library could be a gold mine.

But I missed an obvious problem.

In the 1990s, library music was made entirely on a rig with fake-sounding twentieth-century orchestra samples and soulless drum loops. But I met Mick some twenty years later, when I was in London to record library music with a live orchestra at

Abbey Road Studios, and by then, library music had gotten better, because production costs had come down and the revenue the music generated had shot up. Music libraries had captured a greater share of the market, and better content was being created, generating a sharp rise in demand for high-quality music. Music that used to be dull and insipid was now emotional and exciting. Library music today is written and recorded by world-class composers and orchestras at places like Abbey Road.

Library music had set a baseline of quality and other composers jumped off from there. As libraries began to produce better-sounding music faster, every composer had to keep pace. Today, although library music sounds amazing, custom-composed music sounds even better and is preferred by content creators.

Mick and I could have generated a lot of music very quickly, but without human intervention, it would take about as long to sort through and select the usable outputs and bring them up to modern production standards as it would to write a new piece from scratch. The tide of music quality had risen, and AI music had not risen with it. The technology didn't save work, so it wasn't useful.

For professional composers, generating ideas is easy. Lots of people have good ideas and find novel and ingenious ways to tackle complex problems. What makes musicians professional is not creativity, but craft: a collection of skills and the knowledge of when and how to deploy each one.

Creativity is like water and craft like the vessel that holds it.

BIG QUESTIONS

Without the vessel, water is ubiquitous but not usable. Without water, even the most beautiful vessel is empty.

Finding new and different ways to hone musical ideas into listenable and relatable music is a composer's job, and to accomplish it, a composer needs craft. Automating creativity is like adding more water to the ocean. Currently, AI can produce an endless amount of water, but, so far, no usable vessels. I don't get paid for my ideas. I get paid for my process, which includes my ability to deliver my ideas to a listener.

I learned craft by attending the recording session for Alan Menken's *Tangled* score and working at Remote Control. Mastering the formula for trailers and the clichés to make them work is craft. In my job, creativity is momentary. Craft takes time. Automating creativity is not useful because creativity is not work. The work is in harnessing that creativity and bringing it to market.

Luckily, Mick and I realized this before we got into the project. Since then, several companies have tried to automate library music, and after an initial funding round, they've run into the same problem.

I once asked Mick why he was interested in music technology and artificial intelligence and how his work and expertise in music had led him to become a technologist.

"My primary interest," he said, "is to build new things that make new sounds." He views himself as an instrument maker no differently than if he were building violins or saxophones or bone flutes. He knows about coding and AI models for the same reason I know about networking and the software on my rig: because it helps us make the music we want to make.

How could a technologist, who spends all day writing and thinking about code, be an instrument maker? The evolution of musical instruments, from the bone flute to the rig, resulted from the work of a millennia of instrument builders like Professor Grierson, solving some problems, discovering new ones, then solving those. Instrument makers use whatever technological means are available to create new things that make new sounds. Millennia ago, it was bones; centuries ago, it was wood and steel. Today, it's computer code and electricity.

Scientists and engineers using the available technology made the second half of the twentieth century boom years for music. Soon after Turing conceived of computers, teams around the world, including the scientists at Los Alamos, built them. Today, most people have unlimited access to incredibly powerful machines. If someone like Professor Grierson encounters an interesting problem that can be solved by a billion coordinated Turing machines, he can probably solve that problem before he'll ask himself, or be asked by anyone else, if it's a problem he should solve.

Because Mick's work no longer has to happen in a physical domain where wood needs to cure and metal needs to harden, he can create new sounds and new ways to make sounds as quickly as his imagination will allow. In the same way that a composer can use a rig to make any music they can imagine, Mick can use his machines to help imagine new ways to make new sounds.

BIG QUESTIONS

The limitations of the physical world no longer apply to music-making or sound creation. A composer is constrained only by their imagination (or the instrument maker's) and an audience's tolerance for new sounds. We haven't begun to explore the upper bounds of those limitations. The rig is still so new that its implications have yet to be fully realized. Rigs are digital representations of the analog machines used for music creation in the same way that computer keyboards were modeled after their analog counterpart, typewriters. But they don't have to be, and I suspect that new, more efficient interfaces will soon be invented.

It took me years to learn that finding new sounds is the name of the game. New sounds make composers distinctive and empower them to discover their voices. Now that each composer has their own rig, each made of more or less the same hardware, new sounds and musical ideas are what set composers like Hans Zimmer apart from their competitors.

New sounds made Lorde's voice famous. If I had to give an elevator pitch for the history of music, I'd call it, "the search for new sounds."

If music history is the story of the search for new sounds, artificial intelligence is the story of the search for new ways to process data. Where sounds become data is where the threads of these stories weave together into something predictable but totally unexpected.

Mick's AI model wouldn't help us automate the creation of top-quality library music, but with a lot of human collaboration, it could help us finish Schubert's Unfinished Symphony. Several years after he and I first met, just a few miles away from Mick's London office, executives were discussing a project that would need that very capability.

Huawei is the largest manufacturer of mobile phones in the world, but their phones aren't available in the US, so when I first learned about the Unfinished Symphony project, I hadn't heard of them. They'd tasked their European public relations firm, Red Consultancy, with finding innovative ways to announce new products.

In 2018, Huawei was working on the launch of a new flagship phone, the Mate 20 Pro, which would be equipped with a new microchip they called "the AI chip." It was an impressive release, and they were looking for a way to demonstrate the phone's substantial capabilities. Usually, PR firms use elaborate pitch decks to present projects and campaigns. Before a client approves a marketing concept, they're shown projections and digital mockups. The team at Red Consultancy brainstormed hundreds of possible marketing campaigns and made many detailed presentations, but the best marketing ideas are often the simplest.

During the brainstorming and presentation phase, someone at Red sent a one-line email that read, "Why don't we use AI on the Mate 20 Pro to finish Schubert's Unfinished Symphony?"

Ed Staples, a charming, unpretentiously brilliant British man, had worked for Red Consultancy for decades. When he received the email, he immediately forwarded it to Rosie

BIG QUESTIONS

Bannister, who handled communications at Huawei's UK office. She loved the idea, and based on that single sentence, the project was approved.

Ed turned to Denzil Thomas, a man who has worn nearly every hat in the music business, from performer to beer distributor at concerts. At the time, Denzil was a principal at a company called Bronze Format, which could create an endlessly evolving custom mix of any song using AI. Ed forwarded the one-sentence pitch to Denzil, and Denzil forwarded it to Mick Grierson, who just happened to be chief technologist at Bronze Format. (I mention all these people, and there are too many more to mention them all, because before a note of music was written by an AI or a human, a few dozen people were involved in this process.)

As a musician and technologist, Mick knew all the best composers in London and could have asked any of them to do this project. In late 2018, he mentioned the project to me, and I told him I was very interested. I initially thought he called me first because of the work we'd done on our AI Music Library idea, but he later told me that he just felt I'd be open to the idea. I don't have a classical music background, but I'm capable of commanding an orchestra, and I was glad to try something out of the ordinary. He thought I had the skill to pull it off and wouldn't have moral objections to letting a machine tinker with the work of an immortal musical genius like Schubert.

While Mick and Denzil were working out the details, Ed and Rosie were planning the event. They chose a date in early February of 2019 to coincide with the phone's launch. My CV circulated among the many decision-makers, and on the fourth of January, 2019, the corporate machinery spit out a "Yes."

By that time, the concert date was only a month away. Even the real Schubert might not have been able to write half a symphony that fast.

A month on paper was only about two weeks in practice, because the music would have to be passed on to a human orchestrator and then a copyist before the first rehearsal. A performance of a symphony in a concert hall is an entirely different undertaking than sight-reading film music in a recording session. There is no "take two" in a performance, and once the music is on paper, it's very difficult to make more than a minor change.

I needed to get familiar with the AI on Huawei's new phone and wrap my mind around the enormity of the task. The logistics were mind-bendingly complicated. I approached the project less like a musician and more like a technologist.

How could I get all this music written and into the production pipeline in the time allowed? No one on Red Consultancy's production team had produced an orchestral concert before, so Denzil and I would have to walk them through the very specific logistics. Even more terrifying, like almost all contemporary composers, I'd never written a symphony. Schubert would provide source material, and AI would help, but I'd have to put it all together, and if it went badly, the rotten tomatoes would be thrown at me.

Very early on in the project, I anthropomorphized the AI by naming it "Pierre," after a character in a Jorge Louis Borges story

BIG QUESTIONS

I'd read as a child. (I'll explain in the final chapter of this book why that name and story were particularly appropriate for the Schubert project.) I thought of the machine as a colleague, an assistant who never got tired or needed a break. It wasn't actually a machine at all but a program, an algorithm. It was an early AI model called an LSTM, or Long Short-Term Memory. This model could be trained and prompted with audio recordings and would generate an output of new audio based on its training material. It didn't have a real user interface, so I had to send the training data and prompts to an engineer who would then interact with the model and send me the outputs via email. It seems medieval by today's standards, but this was cutting-edge just a few years ago.

We trained the AI on audio recordings of all Schubert's music, then prompted it with the first two movements of the unfinished eighth symphony. The results sounded like cats walking on a piano. This changed the way I thought about music. I immediately understood why the AI had delivered such a haphazard output: training on just audio recordings of a symphony and then asking for a similar output is like training on photos of building facades and asking the AI to design an interior. Without context, like knowledge of the building's use and the importance of certain features, how could any system draw correct conclusions? I viewed these first outputs as a failure on my part to explain the goals of the project. I'd taken too much of my musical knowledge for granted—knowledge that neither the AI or its programmers possessed.

I decided to think of the AI as a skilled professional to whom I'd given bad instructions. So we gave it new training data—Schubert's melodies instead of his full symphonies—and asked it to give us simple melodies back. This time, what it generated sounded like music, but the melodies were twenty or thirty years too modern for Schubert.

I felt the AI had developed some understanding of Schubert's predicament. It's entirely plausible that he had painted himself into a corner with his Eighth Symphony and failed to finish it because the stylistic constraints of his time made it difficult for him to see a way forward. The symphony was brilliant but ahead of its time, surprising even Schubert's ears. The Eighth has a more modern, harmonically daring sound than his other symphonies. He wrote two movements and a sketch of a third (which we decided not to use in creating the full third movement), and all the movements were in triple meter, which had never been done in a symphony. I theorized that had he lived, he might have returned to this piece later in life and finished it at a time when he would have been on the cusp of musical modernity, ushering in a new era of possibility for the symphonic form. If syphilis and mercury poisoning hadn't killed him at an impossibly young age and he premiered a finished Eighth, it might have been the first in a new class of modern symphonies.

Schubert scholars have disagreed with me. And there's not much point in speculating about what a composer might have done if he'd lived longer. Even if we somehow managed to resurrect a digital Schubert, how could we know that what we constructed was anything like the original? Perhaps we could train an AI with all of his music, omitting the last movement of one of his completed symphonies. Then we could prompt this AI Schubert with other movements of the same symphony to see if it finished that symphony in the same way the living Schubert had.

I haven't heard of anyone conducting an experiment like this, probably because it would obviously fail. If we did somehow create a computer program that was Franz Schubert, or if we resurrected the man himself through science or sorcery, how he finished his symphony would depend on his experience up until the moment he put pen to paper. Music is not the solution to an equation. It's a process.

If we could resurrect Schubert's consciousness, the experience of having been dead and now alive centuries later would be destabilizing and profoundly affect his process. So even if this "real" Schubert had written the last two movements of the symphony himself, they would not be the same movements he would have written had he lived to finish the piece in his old age. Nor would they be what he would have written had he finished the Eighth Symphony in the days or weeks after he started it.

There is no one "right" answer to the question "How would Schubert have finished his Unfinished Symphony?" There are an infinite number of right answers.

The AI created a long stream of melodies. Initially, I just listened to each and made a note if a particular one stood out for some reason. Some of these melodies were too complicated for the style, others were too simple, but a few stood out as rich symphonic themes—the kind Schubert might have invented. Once I had extracted what I considered the best possible outputs from the AI, I set up a call with Red Consultancy and Huawei to tell them how I planned to finish the project. Originally, they had wanted the AI running on their phone to do all the creative work. I think they imagined my role as some kind of supervisor. I told them that wouldn't work, that the project was much more profound. It would be a collaboration between a human composer and an AI. The AI would interpret Schubert's body of work and generate melodies that he might have used, and I, the human, would do the complicated work of weaving those into a symphony and collaborating with the conductor and the orchestra to bring that symphony to life.

Giving voice to everyone's main objection, Rosie asked, "Are we still finishing the symphony with the phone if you're doing some of the writing?"

I told her that machines, even advanced machines like the new Huawei phone, are useless without human users. They're tools that help us with our daily tasks, connecting us and helping us draw insight from the vast amount of data floating around. They exist to save work. I believed, and still believe, that using a machine to finish Schubert's Eighth Symphony would be impossible without human intervention. I also believed it would be meaningless.

It might be possible to create a Rube Goldberg assembly of software and hardware that could write, orchestrate, copy, print, and perform a piece of classical music in the style of any composer, but why? But what's the point, other than to say we did it?

What we could accomplish by collaborating with machines is far more profound and meaningful than what we—or the machines—could achieve alone. Within ten days, we were going to write, rehearse, and perform a symphony with a team dispersed between Los Angeles and London. That alone would have been impossible without the Huawei technology.

That virtual meeting was the first time I'd seen or interacted with Rosie or Ed. Their plan was to have me send the completed symphony to London without flying me over for the premiere. Soon after that virtual meeting, Denzil told me they wanted me to come to London, be the face of the project, and tell anyone who would listen what I'd just told them: that even the most advanced machines are useless without human participation.

To generate the fourth movement, we had to train the AI on Schubert's two existing movements as well as the third movement, which I had completed.* This meant making a MIDI file—

---

* Schubert aficionados have asked me why I didn't simply use the entr'acte from Schubert's incidental music for the play *Rosamunde* as the fourth movement. It is believed by some, within the very narrow and specific corner of musicology that considers such things, to be the piece that Schubert intended as the fourth movement of his Eighth Symphony. The honest answer is that I didn't know about that piece at the time. Had I known about it, I still would have lobbied to write a new movement for the same reason that I decided to ignore Schubert's likely sketch of his third movement. This project was about human creativity and technology and not about academic research and theory.

essentially, musical notation converted into a computer-readable language—of the third movement in a matter of hours. No one at Huawei or Bronze knew about the process for creating realistic demos I'd learned at Remote Control Productions. They didn't know I was writing Schubert's symphony on my rig, whose sole purpose was to make orchestral music digitally, or that I'd been creating the audio demo and the MIDI file as I went along.

I work not by writing notes on paper but by making demos as I go. One thing I realized while finishing the symphony was that creating fully realized music without the intermediary of written notation had become not just a commercial necessity, but an integral part of my process. As I've said, the DAW that I use to write is a musical instrument. It's the instrument that I play. I essentially perform a composition into the DAW, hearing it as I'm creating it. I then have to reverse-engineer my work back into notation. This is not entirely different from how a composer like Schubert would have worked. He would have played his music on a piano, written that music down in notation, and then orchestrated his sketch. My process is just faster.

So, when I got a panicked call from Denzil telling me we needed to make a MIDI file for the AI to write the fourth movement, he was relieved to hear that it was already made. I posted it to the AI team in London before I hung up the phone. The fourth movement was written using the same process as for the third. I sent all the MIDI files to the engineer, got the model's response, arranged the result, sent it to the orchestrator, and then it was time to fly to London for rehearsal.

BIG QUESTIONS

While I was asleep on the plane on my way to London, the orchestrator and copyist finalized the score and created parts for each musician. When I arrived at Abbey Road Studios, I picked up my copy of the score, and for the first time I held the completed symphony in my hands. As the orchestra tuned up and the rehearsal was about to begin, I started to freak out. What if it wasn't good? What if I'd rushed it? What if it was boring? What if it sounded robotic? These pointless ruminations bubbled in my mind like a pot about to boil.

Executives from Huawei and Red Consultancy were strewn about the studio. I met Rosie and Ed in person for the first time, then had a brief discussion with the conductor about last-minute details.

The first two movements are mainstays of the orchestral repertoire, and the musicians in the orchestra had already played them many times. They were anxious to hear the new movements, so the conductor began the rehearsal with movement three.

When he raised his baton to begin, it occurred to me that unlike every film project I'd ever done, no one outside my team had had any input. I'd made a demo to train the AI, but no one had ever heard it. This was the biggest project of my life, and the thing I'd learned to do best—make good demos and collaborate on musical details with non-musicians—was unnecessary. In the past, when I worked on a film, or on Lorde's cover of "Everybody Wants to Rule the World," a director or producer guided me and gave me feedback. I'd had none of that on this project. Anything wrong with this music was one hundred percent my fault.

The executives at Red Consultancy were hoping to impress the executives at Huawei, and the executives at Huawei were understandably curious about what they'd purchased and would spend lavishly to promote. It all rode on my work, which no one, including me, had heard performed by humans.

I'd never even heard the orchestration. I knew that Brad Dechter, the orchestrator for this project, was a master, and I'd reviewed the score, but he'd made a few changes since I last saw it. What if something was wrong? What if some Huawei executive was also a Schubert fanatic and didn't like what I did with the piece? I couldn't do anything to change it, even if I wanted to. I was in London, away from my rig and my team, at Abbey Road Studios, a cathedral to recorded music where a symphony I'd written with artificial intelligence would be heard by human ears for the first time.

Everyone in the room was dead silent. You could have heard, well, a mouse fart. Then the orchestra began to play. I was looking at the musician's faces to see how they felt. They'd know from the first measures if the newly completed third movement was good.

A violinist once told me that playing a beautiful symphony in an orchestra feels like flying. I've seen orchestras struggling, and I've seen them flying. When they feel they're flying, they relax, and the music flows out.

I scanned the faces of the first violins on the left all the way to

BIG QUESTIONS

"It's proper music!" Dom Kelly (*right*) and me during a rehearsal for the finished symphony. PHOTOGRAPH BY ARCHIE BROOKSBANK @BLADESMAN_

the cellos on the right. They were all flying. They all understood the project. Some had probably come into the room feeling antagonistic toward the very idea. But here they were playing it, and I could tell they liked it.

Apart from my library music, our orchestra contractor, Dom Kelly, had never heard my work, and I think he was skeptical that I could write a symphony. Just a few bars in, he turned to me with a surprised look face and said, "It's proper music!" We both laughed out loud, and I saw some of the musicians crack a smile as though they realized the same thing at the same moment.

There were problems with the first take. There usually are. The conductor stopped to clarify a few things and made some decisions about bowing and other important details. I was so lost in those details with him and so engrossed in the joy of bringing music to life, I almost forgot about the clients who, I thought, would also have notes on what they were hearing.

I looked at Rosie and Ed, who were sitting with a few of their colleagues and clients. They all had the same expression on their faces. It was the expression I'd had when I stood up in the middle of Alan's recording session for *Tangled*—pure, childlike amazement.

I was so stressed, I'd totally forgotten the power of a live symphony orchestra. For a moment, I got to hear the piece and to see the scene through their eyes. I'd been so focused on the details, I'd forgotten to appreciate the magnitude of being at Abbey Road Studios. The building itself is hallowed ground.

On top of that, a symphony orchestra was playing a composition co-written by artificial intelligence that had run on a mobile phone. The magnitude of the moment gave me the confidence to go to them, and like a waiter inquiring about a dish he knows is delicious, I asked, "How are you enjoying your symphony?" They were British, and they smiled, almost broadly, and nodded in my direction, which I think translates into American as falling over themselves in fulsome praise.

As the rehearsal went on, executives began to filter out of the room. I think most of them showed up to make sure the concert they'd heavily promoted wouldn't be a total disaster. Hearing the orchestra play the third movement had been enough to satisfy their curiosity.

BIG QUESTIONS

From my perspective, rehearsals never go well. The music is never exactly as I imagined it. Of course it isn't. It's being performed by humans. It's alive. When people play it, it takes on a life of its own. A good performance is like seeing your child as an adult, but a rehearsal, even a good one, is more like seeing the kid as an awkward teenager. Although the rehearsal seemed like a disaster to me, Julian Gallant, the conductor, told me that it went well. Still, I spent the days between the first rehearsal at Abbey Road and the concert scrutinizing the score and agonizing over details I couldn't change. The artist Roy Lichtenstein once remarked, "Every artist dreams of sneaking into the museum and finishing their painting." Every piece I've ever written, in its own way, is unfinished.

I went over every interaction I'd had at the first rehearsal and wondered whether I'd done or said something wrong, made the wrong joke to the wrong person. Maybe I'd spent too much time talking to one person at the expense of another. In short, I had a slow and steady panic attack that lasted a few days.

This piece would be premiered at Cadogan Hall, one of the most revered classical music venues in the world. It would be scrutinized by tech journalists, and no matter how it came out, it would almost certainly draw some hate from classical music enthusiasts.

The day of the concert, I arrived at a hotel near the venue where a press junket was set to begin. Rosie met me at the door and took me straight into an interview with Andy Boxall, a feature writer from the online magazine *Digital Trends*. Andy was dressed casually but sharply, and he exuded friendliness and curiosity. He asked a few questions about me, then asked the question that seemed to have been burning in his—and everyone else's—mind.

"So," he said. "Who put the emotion in the symphony, you or the AI?"

For reasons I didn't understand until years later, his question annoyed me a little. It made me think of whiny singer-songwriters trying to elicit big emotions from awkward teenagers. For some reason, I thought of Jeff Buckley's cover of Leonard Cohen's "Hallelujah." To me, the answer was so obvious I felt a little silly saying it.

I'd spent the past eight years or so making music for media. Emotion is what a media composer adds to a production. I'd written happy music while in a terrible mood and terrifying music while in a great mood. I don't need to think about my own state of mind when trying to elicit emotion in music. When I write music, I'm thinking about the people who will listen to it and about the context in which they'll hear it. I try to inhabit their state of mind as much as possible, then write what I think will elicit the desired feelings. So, the knee-jerk reaction is that the emotion comes from me.

But it doesn't really come from me. It comes from centuries, maybe millennia, of convention, catalogued into a unidirectional language by the musicians who have come before me. This language is composed of everything from familiar clichés to general rules a composer can combine to elicit a reliable emotional response from an audience.

It works in film, when emotions are being manipulated by narrative, images, and sound. In a concert hall, only sound is on display. How will the audience react to it emotionally? I had some hunches, but I didn't really know. This is why premieres are so exciting. No one, including the musicians and the composer, know how the audience will react. It's a tightrope act and the only possible outcomes are success or certain death.

So, who put the emotion in the music, me or the AI?

"Neither," I told Andy. "The emotion doesn't come from me, it doesn't come from Schubert, and it doesn't come from an AI. It comes from you. You're the one who will feel something or not, and the experience of a concert is different for every audience member."

At a concert you experience something with a group of people, and then you talk about your individual experience and compare it with theirs. Each individual interpretation can add context, not just about the performance but about the person doing the interpreting. If the emotion came from the composer, there'd be no need to discuss music at all. Everyone who heard the music would experience it in the same way.

The valence of music is open and personal because it's so abstract. It's communication without words or pictures. It's sounds whose meanings are dependent on context. On their own, they have no specific meaning at all.

Andy and I discussed this idea for a few minutes, then

the next group came into the room. They were reporters from several Spanish news outlets. One reporter, whose name I never learned, spoke first: "Should we be using this kind of technology to create art? Don't we lose something when we turn our jobs over to technology?" Only a few years later, his questions seem quaint.

I looked around the room and noticed that some of the reporters had cameras. Most had Huawei phones out and ready to record. Only one reporter had a notepad. I theatrically gestured to all the technology and waited for them to notice the irony of questioning the use of technology in my line of work when it was so prevalent in theirs. It took a moment, but they acknowledged it with an appropriately subdued chuckle.

I asked, "Anyone going to hand-write this article and have a courier bring it to their editor? Technology is already an indispensable part of our lives. You use it in your job, and I use it in mine. Today, music, and every other form of art, is made and distributed with digital technology. A hit song no longer exists solely as a physical product. Recording technology has ushered in the most fertile century in music's history. Collaborating directly with artificial intelligence is an impressive step, but it's just one in a series of small steps we've taken throughout history."

The Spanish journalists peppered me with personal questions to get "color," then Rosie whisked me upstairs to a room that looked like, and probably had been, a Victorian library. It was filled with light-hearted but serious Dutch journalists, whose questions seemed philosophical but were essentially the same ones I'd already answered—variations on "Who put the emotion in the music?" and "Should we be using this kind of technology to create art?" My answers were translated into dozens of languages that day. One Dutch travel reporter asked what kinds of pants I like to wear on an airplane. I think there's an article on my travel habits in a Dutch magazine somewhere.

After the interviews, I was escorted to the concert hall where the final rehearsal was already underway. I sat in the audience listening for every nuance, scribbling on my score, making notes. I was freaking out, but I was the only one. Everyone else in the ensemble thought it was going very well. Over the years, I've learned that my feelings about a rehearsal of my music are not a reliable indicator of how well the piece will turn out. The musicians were happy. The conductor was happy. The best thing I could do was let them work.

When the conductor turned to ask if I had any notes, I said, "I've been talking to reporters all day and I'll be talking to them until showtime to tell them how amazing you guys sound. It's a relief to hear that I haven't been lying to the press." I thanked them for their hard work and gave, more or less, the speech I'd heard Alan Menken give before the *Tangled* session. After another round of interviews while the rehearsal wound up and the musicians got dressed and ready for the concert, I was hustled to the wing on stage right, where I was confronted by a friendly but serious Chinese man flanked by bodyguards.

Rosie brought me forward and said, "This is Walter Ji,

president of Huawei Europe." Walter oversaw a market worth billions of dollars, and his group, Huawei Europe, had paid for and arranged the event.

I wondered why he'd chosen to meet me backstage and found out that he was planning to introduce the concert personally.

After an engaging introduction, Walter came offstage, and I went on to participate in a panel discussion with the evening's host, English musician and TV presenter Myleene Klass; Huawei's Head of Handsets, Arne Herkelmann; and Huawei's Chief Brand Officer, Andrew Garrihy. We talked briefly about the new phone, the technology, and the creative process.

"Do you think AI is good for music?" Myleene asked.

I looked out at Cadogan Hall, packed to the rafters with influencers and tech journalists, and realized this was the youngest classical music audience I'd ever seen. I asked, "How many of you have been to the symphony before?" About two thirds of the audience, more than I expected. "How many have you have heard Schubert performed live?" A few people clapped and I laughed in disbelief. "And how many of you have heard Schubert performed live but aren't my guests or guests of the orchestra?" The room was silent, then rolled into a communal chuckle.

"We can speculate about the long-term implications of this project, but the immediate impact is that you're all going to enjoy a part of our shared human heritage that you might not have had the opportunity to enjoy otherwise. If AI can make young people enthusiastic about Schubert, that's a win."

BIG QUESTIONS

I heard a knowing grumble of approval and the sound of thousands of social media posts being created at once.

Myleene asked, "What was it like writing this symphony with AI?"

In a previous interview, I'd said that working with the AI was like having an assistant who never got tired and never took a break. Rosie liked that soundbite, so I used it a few more times. It's the way junkets go: you find something that works and stick with it.

"I'll add that the most nerve-wracking part of this project was knowing that a piece I completed would be performed on the same program as Schubert's work. Regardless of the role of the AI, this score has my name on it. It's like watching the greatest comedian in the world do a half-hour set of material before someone hands you the mic. You might not be able to tell, but I'm extremely nervous right now."

This got a bit of a laugh, and Myleene, who has a performer's sense of showmanship, wisely wrapped up the interview on a high note.

When I walked into the wings, one of Walter's bodyguards was waiting for me. "Walter would be honored if you and your friends would sit beside him."

"Of course," I said, and followed him through the bowels of the theater to the balcony.

All that was left was to listen to about twenty minutes of authentic Schubert before the biggest piece I'd ever written was performed. I sat between my father-in-law and my best friend

The orchestra at London's Cadogan Hall, about to begin the third movement. PHOTOGRAPH BY ARCHIE BROOKSBANK @BLADESMAN_

Matt, who'd flown from the US for the premiere. Walter Ji, one of the most powerful men in the world, was right in front of us with his entourage.

While I had been in the backrooms and hallways of Cadogan Hall earlier, giving interviews, Red's creatives had been producing an elaborate but subtle light show to accompany the symphony. When the second movement ended, the lights changed, and some began to glow Huawei Red. It was time for the AI portion of the show.

As the conductor raised his baton to begin the third movement, I leaned over to Walter and said, "I hope you enjoy your symphony."

While working on the symphony, my only concern had been that it would be entertaining and rousing. I imagined those last two movements moving the audience to laughter, contemplation, and, ultimately, a standing ovation. I wanted them to be moved to applaud between movements, which is rarely done at classical music concerts, even if they politely resisted the urge. The AI supplied some of the melodic material, Schubert had provided some as well, and what I deemed necessary to connect the two and make them seem like a unified idea had been my human contribution.

Going into the project, I knew that expectations for the symphony's musical integrity were low. No one thought that an AI could write a symphony, so whatever it came up with would be impressive. I also knew that, from the perspective of an audience member, the novelty would be entertaining for a few seconds at best. I needed to make the symphony a show that an audience of mostly classical neophytes would enjoy. I also needed to make it a piece the musicians would find challenging but not so challenging they couldn't pull it off after only two rehearsals. They needed to be surprised, but not too surprised.

I'd talked with Huawei, Red, and the tech team at Bronze Format about the particulars of how to extract the right melodies from the data sets and how to better train the AI, and I'd had more important conversations with Brad Dechter, the lead orchestrator, about how to make the symphony into a show.

When I invite any audience to hear my music, I want them to arrive expecting a concert and to leave having seen a show. This means the performance has to include at least three things: a heartfelt moment, a laugh, and a surprise. In a less formal concert, when I play an instrument and introduce the program personally, I can usually take care of one or two of these ingredients with patter or some kind of sideshow. I once produced a concert in which zombies came down the aisles and dragged the conductor off the stage while he was conducting the music from the TV show *The Walking Dead*. That stunt served as both a laugh and a surprise.

For a classical symphony in the style of Franz Schubert, there's no talking between movements, no sideshows, and certainly no zombies. Everything had to be written into the score. How could I use music to convey those three elements? I knew the audience would have expectations formed by lifelong exposure to culture and cliché. I could either fulfill those expectations or artfully break them.

The heartfelt moment in the concert would simply be the moment Dom and I had shared in the first rehearsal: the realization that this was "proper music," indistinguishable from music written entirely by a human. The audience at Cadogan Hall was hearing this hybrid human-machine composition for the first time, which, in itself, would inspire collective reflection. Everyone in the room knew something important was happening.

The surprise in the piece was easy to add. Almost by definition, symphonies are full of surprises. A familiar melody from another movement is reprised. The orchestration suddenly drops to a single instrument, then explodes into an exciting full ensemble. A clever change in harmony jolts the listeners' expectations. Because the genre is so well-defined, surprise—breaking conventions or turning them on their heads—makes the music interesting.

The laugh was the hardest thing to fit into the piece, and I did this simply by refusing a surprise in one section. I had to manufacture this element myself.

Classical music is one of the only types of performance where the audience shows up not expecting to laugh. Laughter is involuntary, joyous, one of the oldest human responses. It's primal and it builds community. Laughter is also the most difficult response to elicit from an audience without the aid of narrative. How do you tell a musical joke everyone will understand?

I think one reason classical concert music is waning in popularity is that it's no longer participatory. If you're playing music in a club, the audience gives you feedback in real time. They cheer, or they lose interest and start chatting. In some clubs, bad solos are even jeered. When the audience likes what they hear, they urge you on.

Classical music used to be that way. If they liked it, audiences would clamor for an aria from an opera or even a movement of a symphony to be reprised. If it was met with enough applause, orchestras would sometimes play the same movement twice. I think that's much more fun for both audience and performer. But classical music has changed from an exercise in entertainment to an exercise in perfection. Today, if you like a movement of a symphony, you don't need the orchestra to play it again; you can listen to it in the car on the way home, while in Schubert's time, the audience probably wouldn't have had an opportunity to hear the piece again in their lifetimes.

Modern technology has brought recorded music much closer to perfection. Musicians are technically far better today than they were in Schubert's time, and contemporary audiences go to the symphony expecting to hear a live performance close to the near-flawlessness they hear on recordings. This pushes musicians' technical capabilities and moves the art form forward. But I don't think it's as interesting. I like to write music that reminds the audience it's supposed to be fun.

In the fourth movement of the completed symphony, I begin with a long, jaunty melody played by the entire string section plucking their strings. It builds to a frantic crescendo, indicating that something intense and serious is coming. Then the section suddenly repeats; just when you'd expect to be swept into serious reverie, you're back at the beginning of the silly melody. Apologies to the readers of this book who have not listened to the symphony. I don't know if explaining the "joke" will diminish its effectiveness. Maybe that makes it even funnier.

In the moments leading up to the performance, I fixated on the fourth movement joke, convinced, rightly or wrongly, that the audience's enjoyment hinged on that comedic moment. At the premiere, a few moments before the music arrived at the punchline, the audience seemed to lighten up. The sonority of pizzicato strings made them a little happier.

I felt Walter Ji stir when the strings plucked the carefree

melody. Everyone around me seemed to move slightly to the beat, trying to anticipate where it might go next.

When the section repeated, I heard a suppressed chuckle. The audience wanted to laugh, but they thought it was inappropriate. Because everyone had the same reaction, it was even funnier. That was the moment when I knew that all my work, and the work of the AI team, the orchestra, the orchestrators, and the stage crew had paid off. The big, traditional finale would dazzle them, but we'd made them chuckle. It was an emotion they hadn't expected, and it would stay with them long after the final note.

After the comical section, the fourth movement becomes more serious, reprising themes from the previous three movements and building steadily toward the finale. Another AI-generated melody takes the lead, and the symphony Schubert never completed ends with the drama and fanfare typical of the composer and his time. False endings cascade over one another as the entire orchestra plays rich harmonies, dripping with finality but turning back just before the resolution, until the last chord finally lands.

After the final note, there was a pause before the applause began. The audience had been teased with false endings for several minutes, so it took them a few seconds to process what they'd heard and to read the conductor's body language.

For two seconds, the hall was dead silent. For me, that two seconds was an eternity. Even as I write this, a small part of me is still sitting there in abject horror, wondering why no one is clapping.

The applause began slowly and grew louder. Walter stood up and then everyone else got to their feet. I heard "Bravo!" and even some whistling. The standing ovation was as sweet as the moment of silence that preceded it had been terrifying. Artificial intelligence had made its concert debut, and the audience had enjoyed the show. Whether the emotion came from the audience, me, Schubert, or the AI, it was palpable.

In the days that followed, I was surprised by the positive reviews. I shouldn't have been. Huawei had rolled out the red carpet for so many journalists and the piece was enjoyable, if nothing else. Andy Boxall's feature was glowing and reflected the warmth and insight I'd felt during our conversation. I don't know how it played in the Spanish, German, or Dutch press, but I was told it was largely positive.

We did it. But what had we done?

WHAT WE DID

Sometimes, to interact with technology, we need to anthropomorphize it. When a computer or mobile phone is slow to load something important, it can feel personal and intentional, even though we know it's not. Many apps respond to "rage shakes" by asking if there's something wrong with the app's performance. I think everyone knows that shaking your phone will not enhance its performance, but we do it so often that programmers have learned to use it as an indication of the user's state of mind.

In the time when the first bone flute was made, and probably stretching millions of years before that, some humans assumed that a sound in the bushes was alive and possibly malevolent, while others were more skeptical and logical. Relaxed vigilance rarely has consequences, but when it does, they can be catastrophic, so evolution selected the more vigilant of the species, who survived to become our ancestors. To assume that something non-human has sophisticated, malevolent intentions served our ancestors well and was probably passed down to us.

Our consciousness has evolved to allow us to imagine what it's like to become someone else, but we haven't lost the instincts of creatures of prey. We imagine there is a conscious, intelligent, intentional agent behind everything, even when there isn't, as in the case of our smartphones.

Anthropomorphizing technology may not be a useful cognitive tool, but it's our default position, and it may take conscious effort to overcome it. The more interactive tech becomes, the more difficult it is to overcome the feeling that it's thinking. Which is why Turing Tests and other benchmarks exist. Our default position is to believe that machines are intelligent and that, in time, their intelligence will blossom into consciousness. Maybe this will happen, but to believe it's inevitable is closer to religion than science.

It's almost impossible to conceptualize a product a computer might produce without imagining it was produced intentionally. This is clearer than ever today as more and more people interact with GPTs as if they were friends, advisors, even therapists. In the case of a symphony, it's even difficult to describe the project without making the computer a character with a conscious will.

So, it's no surprise that a reporter wrote the headline "Schubert's Unfinished Symphony Is Finished with AI." And it's even less surprising that the article treats the headline's misleading premise as a given.

We simply used AI to analyze a large amount of musical data and make some deductions and inductions. Then I used my power of abduction to set the results in what I thought was an appropriate musical context. I guessed how these melodies might be both faithful to the style of the nineteenth century and entertaining to an audience in 2019.

I used a new musical tool in a new way that allowed me to create a musical, human-sounding piece. Contemporary AI systems are not capable of *understanding* anything, but they are unfathomably powerful tools for furthering human understanding. If we focus too much on computers as consciousness, we'll miss the big picture, which is that computers give conscious humans incredible power.

Although we finished Schubert's Unfinished Symphony with artificial intelligence, what that looked like in practice and what it might look like in the imagination of people who grew up with the stories of Isaac Asimov, *The Terminator*, and the AI evangelism of Elon Musk and Ray Kurzweil are two very different things.

We used AI to reproduce some of Schubert's stylistic features based on his extensive body of work. Because Schubert was exceptionally prolific, he was a prime candidate for this. He was also peripatetic and short-lived, leaving several projects incomplete. From the perspective of computer science, he created a lot of incomplete data sets. But in the words of Mick Grierson, "The idea that successfully extrapolating and reproducing some of Schubert's stylistic elements carries with it some form of awareness or inspiration is just a fallacy."

Many details about music can be described by math, but simple intuition leads us to believe that there's more to it than that. Music is not just mathematical relationships between notes. Those relationships produce sounds, and, like spoken language, those sounds have meaning to humans who understand them.

Music can be *described* by math, but it's not math. No one would argue that thoughts are just combinations of letters, even though many thoughts, including the thoughts in this book, can be described with combinations of letters.

In true mystic fashion, Pythagoras fused music and mathematics in Western minds. Over the past 2,500 years, as we've found more ways to abstract music the way we abstract math, the comparison has grown stronger. We can represent music—sounds in the air—as markings on a page. And in that form, we can study and manipulate music with a depth and breadth that was impossible before written notation. This makes music seem even more like math.

With the Pythagorean idea in the back of our minds that "everything is number," we look for the similarity and find it.

The first and largest step in connecting music to math was to give it its own written symbolic language. In the next chapter, we'll turn our attention next to how sounds became a written abstraction.

III

Scherzo

COWS, DNA, AND THE MAN OF THE MILLENNIUM

COUNTING WITH YOUR HANDS

Before it could be written down, music was just kind of . . . around. It floated aimlessly in human communities like protein molecules in the primordial soup before they congealed into the patterns we call DNA. In this early phase of music, everyone probably knew a few songs, but they didn't try to write them down because they had bigger problems—for example, "How do we keep track of all these cows?"

Let's imagine, in Mesopotamia, sometime thousands of years before the events in the Hebrew Bible, an unknown herdswoman stretching out her hands and beginning to study them. She has no concept of writing, but she thinks her hands might help solve the problem of counting a herd of cows larger than ten. Her solution is still with us today, and it involves complicated math every human on Earth knows intimately. We know it so well, in fact, that it probably doesn't even seem like math.

"Base sixty math" sounds like something calculus grad students use to solve esoteric equations, but we all use it every day, every hour, every second. Most of us have grown so accustomed to the sixty-minute hour and the sixty-second minute we've never wondered why we use this bizarre system to measure time.

The answer is cows.

Our Mesopotamian herdswoman looks at her left hand and notices that each of her four fingers has three sections between the joints. Using her left thumb, she touches each of the three sections on her left forefinger. That's three. Then she does the same on her left middle finger. Six. Then on her other two fingers. Twelve. Then she lifts her *right* thumb to mark twelve and starts over. The first section on her index finger is now thirteen, the second is fourteen, and so on. Using this method of counting sections with her left thumb, and using each finger of her right hand to represent another group of twelve, she eventually extends all the fingers on her right hand to represent five twelves, or sixty.

That's how the Mesopotamian cultures of Sumer and Akkad counted. All their math was based on the "natural" number sixty. It seemed so natural, Egyptian horologists used it on the first sundials. We still use this millennia-old Mesopotamian sixty-digit system, measuring time the way Mesopotamians measured cows.

Mechanical clocks and watches can only be practically and

COWS, DNA, AND THE MAN OF THE MILLENNIUM

efficiently constructed to measure regular increments of time. Unfortunately, Earth doesn't move with mechanical precision. A twenty-four-hour day should be 86,400 seconds long, but depending on geological factors like the tidal deceleration of Earth's spin, a day really lasts between 86,399 and 86,401 seconds. This seems minor, but over long periods, tiny imperfections compound.

We've decided that there are 86,400 seconds in a day, and that each second must be exactly the same length, which means that we have to reset our clocks fairly often to account for the approximation. It's yet another imperfectly solved problem, another instance when we've accepted regularity and consistency at the price of accuracy. This kind of imprecision can also be found in musical scales and in almost every other field, because when we try to capture nature with numbers, nature doesn't quite fit.

We didn't always accept these solutions. As we've seen, our ancestors lived with imprecision. The Romans, for example, didn't use the mechanical dead reckoning of elapsed seconds to calculate time but relied on the position of the sun. They counted twelve hours between sunrise and sunset, and the length of an hour varied from one season to the next. In the summer, an hour was about seventy-five minutes, while in the winter, it was about forty-five. The Romans conquered the known world and ruled it for centuries without any concept of what we would consider a basic fact: the regular, mechanical passage of time.

A Sumerian herdswoman counted her cows in measures of sixty. An Egyptian horologist imposed that scale on a sundial. A German inventor imposed the sundial scale on the first clock. Now, we keep track of time using the same scale with mechanical precision, inaccurate though the system may be. Time is fluid, but we pretend it's rigid so we can measure it with machines. Artificial intelligence, my Lakota friend Tiokasin Ghosthorse, and I each conceive of time in our own way, because the concept of time is a cultural construct. To record time, Westerners traded nuance and reality for permanence and regularity. Does the same thing happen when we try to notate music?

In medieval Europe, time was a choir director's biggest problem. A new chorister might require a decade to memorize all the songs in the liturgical calendar, and with no consistent method of musical notation, memorization was his only option.

In eleventh-century Tuscany, a choir director named Guido d'Arezzo adapted the Mesopotamian hand-counting method to develop a system to help him commit thousands of hymns to memory. He mapped each pitch on a part of the hand, in the same way our herdswoman used her hands to count cows. The details of his system, the "Guidonian Hand," are lost, but his method of making marks on a five-line staff remains with us and is the foundation of modern musical notation.

(Musically literate readers may be trying to connect the twelve sections of the fingers and the twelve notes of a Western chromatic scale. A connection between these naturalistic dozens is exactly what Pythagoras would expect, but we already know that no such "natural" connection could exist, because the twelve notes of the chromatic scale are an arbitrary approximation we accept in order to fit our music into the technology we use to perform it.)

The Guidonian Hand was designed to use muscle memory to help remember songs. Most instrumentalists rely on practiced motions of the hand to create sounds, and this tactile aid makes memorization much easier because it distributes the information across different parts of the body and brain. Guido's system allowed the hands to do some of the memorizing.

While his system of hand memorizing never caught on, monks began to use Guido's notation system to remember their hand gestures and thus remember the songs. Eventually, they realized they could read the song from a page without the intermediary of hand motions. Guido created two new layers of musical abstraction by accident, but only one of them stuck. His invention, like the god Theuth's invention of writing, had consequences he never could have imagined. One of the most significant innovations in music history, it gave us the ability to abstract music in written form. It allowed us to express musical ideas in previously impossible ways, but it also blinded us to the old avenue of sharing musical compositions: the oral tradition.

Music used to be composed, remembered, performed, and passed down by a group of humans, not a single person. Someone might originate a song around a campfire, and as the group performed it together, the song changed as each individual voice made the song their own.

This phenomenon can be observed today in drum circles, which arise spontaneously all over the world from rural Africa to Venice Beach, California. Participate in a drum circle and you'll feel music evolve in real time as the participants play different but dependent and intertwined music together.

Notation marked the beginning of composer-driven music—music written by individuals and remembered externally, rather than belonging to groups of humans and existing only in their minds. Notation allows a composer's name to be attached to the music, and for both music and composer to transcend a lifetime. Before notation, when music wasn't being performed, it was stored—intangibly, corruptibly, and imperfectly—in individual memories. But we are not as far away from this as we might like to believe. "All Along the Watchtower" was written by Bob Dylan, but it was immortalized in Jimi Hendrix's version. "Hallelujah" is best known as an eerie classic by Jeff Buckley, even though it was originally written by Leonard Cohen. The "definitive" version of a song is often a cover, and although songs can be written down, they are often learned by ear.

Notation did make high-fidelity music copying possible, but it hasn't made "oral" transmission obsolete. If pre-notation music was like floating proteins, written music is like DNA. Any two performances of notated music will be recognizably similar, but no two can be exactly alike. Like Pythagoras's wax seals or

COWS, DNA, AND THE MAN OF THE MILLENNIUM

Plato's struck coins, even something as precisely notated as a symphony will sound different with every performance.

In the early 1100s, a generation after Guido's experiments with notation, the youngest daughter of a minor German nobleman was having visions. She was a sickly but brilliant child who spent her youth indoors. At that time in Germany, the only place for a young woman of noble birth, failing health, and a nimble mind was a convent.

Hildegard von Bingen was a polymath, a composer, a writer, and a mystic, thought to be either possessed or a genius. As a Benedictine abbess, she was the first female composer to write music that is still performed today, because she recorded her compositions using Guido d'Arezzo's system, although the number of copies she could create was limited by the number of people who were willing and able to create the manuscripts by hand.

The chance that her music would survive through the ages with her name attached was better because it was written down, but her musical legacy was fragile. Mold and worms degraded the original manuscripts, so they had to be periodically refreshed and recopied.

During her lifetime, Hildegard was extremely famous, and she might have expected her music to outlive her, but she could never have imagined that two hundred and seventy years after her death, about thirty miles up the Rhine from the city of Mainz, an invention would carry her music across a millennium to our ears today.

FROM GUTENBERG TO GRAMOPHONES

If Hildegard had visited Mainz at that time, she would have found a thriving Jewish academy with scholars to rival her in wit and fame, and a prominent Jewish family living on a hilltop near St. Christopher's Church. The hill, the house, and the family were called "Judenberg," or "Jewish Hill." During the Jewish Diaspora in Europe, this center of European Jewish life was destroyed by pogroms in 1096, 1146, and again in 1282.

In the 1282 pogrom, the families of fifty-four Jewish houses, including the Judenberg house, were displaced and their property was snatched by Catholic authorities. The house ended up in the hands of some of the cardinal's henchmen, who changed its name. Custom dictated that the name of the house would become their family name, and it wouldn't do for a highly placed Catholic family to carry a name like "Jewish-hill." So Judenberg became Gutenberg: "good hill." Over several generations, the house changed hands from one German family to the next, until it became the birthplace of Johannes Gutenburg, whom the British Library has called the "Man of the Millennium"—the inventor of the moveable-type printing press.

No one knows exactly when he was born, but it was probably around 1400. (Gutenberg scholars agree that such an important man should have an easily memorable birth year.) His family was wealthy but not noble, which meant Johannes had to work for a living. He started out in the mirror-making business, but that did not go well. So, he decided to invest his meager fortune

COWS, DNA, AND THE MAN OF THE MILLENNIUM

in a startup. By repurposing a wine press, he gave birth to the defining invention of the next five centuries.

In the fifteenth century, books were luxury objects. For those who could afford them, part of their appeal was that they were crafted by hand, which made them unique. While Gutenberg's Bibles would be produced on the massive scale of a few dozen at a time, they were still extremely expensive, so his clients were nobles who could already afford to buy a hand-copied version. To cater to his clients' expectations, Gutenberg made his Bible look hand-copied, but with a few small details that were impossible to do by hand. He changed just enough to make his product stand out, but not so much that he alienated his customer base. He knew his customers would want to be surprised, but not too surprised.

Borrowing techniques from scribes, he used paper cut to a size that matched the golden ratio, so that the width of the page was .618 times its length. The text was printed in a rectangular block at a scale of .618 relative to the size of the page. The big improvement in the Gutenberg Bible was that the text was justified, which meant that the words on each line were neatly aligned on the left and right sides. When a scribe started a line in a handwritten book, it was very difficult to know where that line would end, so most text was aligned to the left, with the right margin ragged. But by inserting tiny spaces between letters, called "kerning," the text forms a neat margin on both sides.

Gutenberg went a step further. He let characters like hyphens and other punctuation bleed beyond the right margin, giving the

> A look of calculated imperfection: punctuation extending beyond the edge of the margin in a Gutenberg Bible. COURTESY INTERNET ARCHIVE

page a look of calculated imperfection. This tiny detail was so precise, it highlighted the real selling point of a printed Bible: accuracy. Hand-copied books were always riddled with errors—a serious problem in a book as important as the Bible. By using precision printing techniques, Gutenberg signaled to his customers that his Bible was error-free and that each copy was identical.

COWS, DNA, AND THE MAN OF THE MILLENNIUM

Gutenberg had revolutionized precision. He'd found a way to make movable-type letters uniform. This precision helped to transform the minds of medieval Europe, and it helped to bring about some of the most significant movements in history: the Renaissance, the Scientific Revolution, and the Enlightenment. But it took another, less famous, visionary to bring this revolution to music.

Gutenberg had solved many of the problems of mechanically reproducing text, but printing Guido d'Arezzo's system of musical notation required multiple passes on the same page, each of which had to be made with extreme precision. Only a few printers had the proper equipment and skills to print the staff, the notes, and the text flawlessly. The first of these was the Venetian Ottaviano Petrucci.

Petrucci was the first to print new editions annually, becoming what we would now recognize as a music publisher. Because of his innovation and the success of the publishing business model, music by composers like Hildegard von Bingen could be printed in runs of hundreds or thousands. It could travel throughout Europe, and while it was still subject to the whims of damp storage, rough roads, and worms, the sheer volume of copies exponentially increased the chances that it would survive.

Through notation, and then through printing, Hildegard von Bingen's music has outlived her by nearly a thousand years. In that time, an entire industry has evolved. We call it the music business. Before Petrucci, music couldn't be sold at any

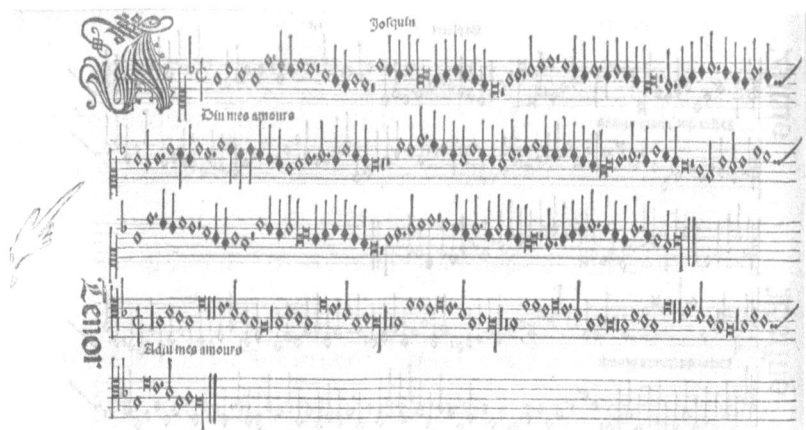

Part of Josquin des Prez's "Adieu mes amours" in Ottaviano Petrucci's *Harmonice Musices Odhecaton*, one of the first instances of sheet music printed with movable type. COURTESY GALLICA DIGITAL LIBRARY/WIKIMEDIA

meaningful scale, but within a generation, it was relatively cheap to produce and in constant demand.

From Petrucci's first printed manuscript to today, composers have been at odds with publishers. Printed music increased the survival chances of all music, but it also kicked off a centuries-long battle for the right to profit from sales and performances. This battle is ongoing, and it has evolved with the technology musicians use. Once we gained the ability to record the actual *sounds* of musical performance, rather than just notating it, the situation became even more complicated.

Thomas Alva Edison was a technophile who tinkered with everything. His early years were spent in nineteenth-century telegraph offices, where he learned the basics of electricity and became an expert in modern communications technology.

COWS, DNA, AND THE MAN OF THE MILLENNIUM

His storied career included the invention of the lightbulb and the formation of the General Electric Company. But the phonograph was his first big hit.

I'm technophilic in my profession, but a luddite in my personal life. I'd rather speak to a human than scroll through a website. Sometimes I even phone my bank, but I still have to navigate their automated menu, or forcefully say "agent" several times until the system relents and puts me in the queue to talk to a human. After I'm forced to listen to looped music, I'm asked to verify personal information and listen to a virtual assistant play it back for me in my own voice.

This is a maddening nuisance, but in 1877, the automated phone system would have sold out concert halls across the country. Edward Johnson, one of Edison's early supporters who became an officer at General Electric, popularized Edison's inventions by holding concerts. In 1878, an evening out might involve Johnson's Telephone and Phonograph Show. Johnson dazzled audiences with a telephone receiver placed on a table onstage. Lively organ music would burst forth, and Johnson would explain that the organist they were hearing was miles away but would take requests by phone. This revelation usually resulted in a standing ovation.

By 1878, when Edison had perfected the phonograph, Johnson finished his concerts by inviting an audience member onstage to sing a song, which he would record on a phonograph, then play back to a stunned and sometimes terrified audience. The effect was even better if the performer was a bad singer whose missed pitches and ear-splitting sonorities were replicated exactly. Like Gutenberg's punctuations outside the margins, the perfectly reproduced imperfections of a singer's voice proved that what seemed like magic was real.

Today, we know that the phonograph doesn't "speak"—it merely repeats. But this wasn't obvious to early audiences. Until the phonograph, speech was an exclusively human activity, and no one had ever heard a human voice whose source wasn't a physically present person.

The phonograph was the first speaking machine, and the press reasoned that if a machine could speak, it wouldn't be long before a more advanced machine could think, rivaling and even overtaking the intellect of its human creators. A search of *New York Times* headlines for the phrase "mechanical brain" yields results dating to 1882. The imminent invention of a thinking machine is a centuries-old media trope that seems to pop up whenever a radical new technology is unveiled.

Like many modern technologists, Edison believed that a mechanical brain was not just possible but inevitable. In 1910, a *New York Times* reporter asked Edison about his thoughts on the soul and the possibility of its immortality. Unsurprisingly, he replied with a technologically appropriate metaphor. Edison believed that the brain was like a machine, and that memory was like a room full of phonograph cylinders. He described the brain as "nothing more than a wonderful meat-mechanism."

Music is just sounds, but we perceive it through several layers of abstraction: notation, physical performance, recording, and so on. Each of these layers is useful, but understanding music and explaining it to technology in the same abstract terms moves us no closer to machine-made music humans will enjoy. The first bone flute makers captured music by creating a tool that could be manipulated with breath and fingers to predictably produce tones. Guido d'Arezzo was able to abstract the sounds of music into markings on a page. Thomas Edison devised a way to capture the sounds that issued from any source, regardless of the techniques used or abstractions employed to create those sounds.

We are told that we live in an exponential age and that our technology is different and more advanced than anything that came before. People in Edison's time felt the same way. We have faster, more capable computers that can perform amazing feats. Some of what our computers can do seems as much like magic to us as the playback of a phonograph did to a Victorian-era audience. But, like Eugene Goostman or my coin trick, the magic only exists in the hands of the artificer and the minds of the audience. Edison began as a tinkerer, and through manipulating physical objects, he invented the most powerful magic of his day.

Of course, Edison wasn't trying to spark a revolution that would change music forever. He didn't care about music. In fact, he was partially deaf. He thought the phonograph would be used by businessmen to record dictation so they could spend less time writing letters—an analog form of voicemail. Rather than send a letter, an executive could record it on a wax cylinder and deliver it by messenger. Phonograph technology was considered a threat to secretaries.

UNFINISHED

The touring Telephone and Phonograph Show was a huge success. Before 1877, no one had ever heard the same sound more than once. Today, the recorded voice is a ubiquitous banality, something my bank uses to punish me for not using their website. But in 1877, it was a terrifying miracle.

As magical as new musical technologies may seem, the necessary abstraction they entail means there is always something left out. A phonograph captures some frequencies well and others poorly or not at all. For example, in the 1920s, the pitches produced by a string bass were not easily captured. So, much of the popular music of that period featured bands with big brass sections. Tubas replaced strings in the bass parts because they could be recorded clearly. And, as we have seen, the banjo enjoyed unmatched popularity around this time because it could be heard over the rest of the band: its frequency range sounded loud on the radio. When the technology improved, the electric guitar replaced the banjo because it could play more expressively in the same frequency range.

By the 1950s and '60s, thousands of people had spent their careers improving recording fidelity and developing new techniques and equipment. Recording became an art unto itself, giving birth to great works of performative and engineering genius by Jimi Hendrix, Pink Floyd, the Beatles, the Who, and Queen. Disco sounds amazing and rich on huge speakers in a nightclub powered by a vinyl record player, but would that kind of music have arisen without technology?

Today, our playback devices have such high fidelity that

almost anything is possible apart from extreme dynamic range. A piece of classical music might have a passage for *pianissimo* solo harp followed seconds later by the full orchestra playing as loudly as possible. On small speakers, like earbuds, this is almost impossible to replicate. The harp will sound too soft or the orchestra too loud. Try listening to Tchaikovsky's *Nutcracker Suite* in your car: you'll have to adjust the volume constantly. Extreme dynamics are powerful in a concert hall, but they don't translate well to recorded music, especially when played through small speakers.

Nonetheless, the impact of recording technology was revolutionary. In the years from 1877 to 1977, music evolved from an ephemeral, live, communal experience to a repeatable, recorded, and solitary one. Everything about the way we create, commercialize, and consume music has changed. Performers who had been rootless nomads became international celebrities whose recordings were heard by millions of people they never met. These disembodied voices became popular entertainment and valuable commodities worldwide.

THE EXPLOSION

When the phonograph was invented, America was a musical backwater. "Good" music was not a subjective term but an academic one, referring to the classical music written by Europeans like Haydn, Mozart, Beethoven, Schubert, Meyerbeer, and Wagner. In the nineteenth century, it was an uncontroversial "fact" that listening to classical music refined one's tastes.

According to thought leaders at the time, the problem was that most Americans didn't have access to "good" music and heard only the artless drivel of popular songs; this supposedly made them less civilized than their European counterparts who, presumably, whistled Schubert's melodies or hummed Wagner while doing household chores. Americans didn't have access to "good" music because they didn't have access to European orchestras.

The phonograph was supposed to change all that. It made the entire country more musically literate by exposing them to music they wouldn't otherwise hear. And they could listen repeatedly, eventually appreciating the nuances and subtlety—or as much of that as the ultra-low fidelity of an early phonograph record conveyed.

Although an American invented the phonograph, his countrymen never developed a widespread taste for "good" music. Perhaps it's no coincidence that many of the most successful composers America has produced have written "popular" music, although the definition of "pop" varies from one decade to the next.

It's impossible to separate the musical innovations of nineteenth- and twentieth-century America from the technical ones. Prior to recorded music, to hear a Schubert symphony, you needed access to a concert hall and sixty-four trained musicians. The phonograph made classical music—and all music—not just accessible but repeatable. Any performance could be recorded, repeated, and analyzed, and this changed

COWS, DNA, AND THE MAN OF THE MILLENNIUM

American music far more than exposure to the European classics.

The next hundred years of recorded music gave birth to jazz, rock'n'roll, disco, EDM, and more. Nearly everything we consider music today owes its lineage to the ability to hear ourselves play and to share our performances. Repeated listening allows styles to develop and grow beyond the lifetime of a specific performer. I learned jazz by listening to John Coltrane, Miles Davis, Wes Montgomery, and Django Reinhardt, all of whom were dead before I ever picked up an instrument.

Music evolves to the level of complexity that can be supported by the technology used to perform and record it. A flutist can execute complex passages faster, higher, and louder than a human voice. A man can memorize thousands of simple chants, but when musical notation became available, music became complex and layered beyond the limits of human memory. When music was printed and shared, musical styles became international and musical practices spread farther than a teacher or performer could travel. When music became recordable, new, previously unimaginable sounds were created. Almost none of the sounds in modern pop music occur in nature. Many are derived from electronic synthesizers whose sounds are limited only by the human imagination.

And when I used AI to finish Schubert's Eighth Symphony, I wrote the music directly into my rig without the intermediary of notation. Because of technology, I can realize music that is orders of magnitude more complex than even that of the most brilliant pre-notation composers. I don't need to use all the available tools all the time, but they have changed the way my mind works.

In the jargon of paleontology, the Cambrian Explosion is the point in the fossil record where an unprecedented number of lifeforms seem to appear out of nowhere. After the invention of the phonograph, music could spread by word of mouth, as massively distributed printed notation, and as audio recordings. If pre-notation music is molecules in the primordial soup, notated music is DNA, and printed music is a multicellular organism, then recording technology is the catalyst for the Cambrian Explosion. Since 1877, music has propagated to such an extent that it is no longer possible for one human being to review all, or even a significant part, of the human musical canon in a single lifetime.

At the time of this writing, the popular streaming service Spotify has a library of more than one hundred million tracks. It would take over seven hundred years of streaming, 24/7, to listen to it all. Music is added at such a ludicrous pace that by the time you finished listening to all hundred million songs (sometime in the twenty-eighth century) there would be billions of songs on the streaming service, and you would only have heard an incredibly small percent of them. All this music is permanent, fixed, and immortal so long as its format can be read.

The phonograph changed music forever and created a business whose product was recordings. Thomas Edison did not see this coming, nor did he relish speculating about what

COWS, DNA, AND THE MAN OF THE MILLENNIUM

his invention might mean for the future of the art it captured. Like contemporary technologists, Edison was more concerned with creating. And like the god Theuth, his only concern was whether a problem could be solved—not whether it *should* be solved, or whether it was even a problem in the first place.

On the other hand, John Phillip Sousa was all too happy to speculate about the future of the music Edison's machines captured. At the turn of the twentieth century, Sousa was the most famous entertainer in America, and we still listen to his music today. He wrote the bombastic, patriotic songs marching bands played on military holidays like the Fourth of July. The popular British comedy show *Monty Python's Flying Circus* used some of Sousa's music for its opening theme. For reasons I don't understand, the British regard marching band music as comedic, while Americans find it stirring.

Sousa did whistle-stop tours around the world, sometimes performing in three different cities in a single day. His private railroad car opened into a stage, and he sometimes played entire concerts without stepping off the train. The sheet music of his compositions was sold internationally.

In 1906, he wrote an op-ed titled "The Menace of Mechanical Music" (he clearly shares my affection for alliteration) decrying the sale of recordings to the public and rhapsodizing about the irreplaceable emotional impact of live performance. His biggest problem with recorded music was not a high-minded concern for musical emotionality but the fact that recordings were owned by the people who recorded them, not the people who wrote the music or performed it. His issue was that he wasn't being paid for the sale of his own music.

Early recording companies didn't view music as property. At that time, the commercial manifestation of music was in the form of printed sheets. Musical sounds were ephemeral, not tangible but floating in the air. These companies believed that the only value was in the technology they used to capture the music and repackage it, as though music was water and they manufactured bottles.

This injustice led Sousa to become one of the founding members of the American Society of Composers, Authors, and Publishers, known today as ASCAP. Sousa used his fame to lobby Congress for the rights of composers to profit from any performances of their music, including recordings and broadcasts. He wanted to establish a precedent of ownership over the tangible property that is a piece of recorded music. Sousa and ASCAP wanted to create another commercial manifestation of music and establish rules for how it could be owned and monetized.

That argument about the division of ownership among the composer, performers, and recording companies continues today. The composer owns the song, but the record company owns the recording of the song. Leonard Cohen owns the rights to the song "Hallelujah," but Columbia Records owns Jeff Buckley's recording of it.

A few years ago, and a century after Sousa's crusade, I was sent along with a delegation from ASCAP to brief Senator

COWS, DNA, AND THE MAN OF THE MILLENNIUM

Dianne Feinstein about the state of the music business. We were lobbying for badly needed legislation that would address giant loopholes in the government's approach to music copyright. All the technology used to create, commercialize, and consume music had changed since the government last visited the subject in the 1940s.

Senator Feinstein was happy to support these reforms, but her staff grilled us, nonetheless. They asked something to the effect of, "Isn't there more music available now than ever before, and isn't the music business making more money than it was before digital downloading? Doesn't that mean you guys are doing better than you were a decade ago?"

It was a reasonable question. There is more music and more money in the business today than at the previous apex in the late 1990s, just before the advent of streaming services. The resulting legislation passed both houses unanimously, but streaming services have found new loopholes to exploit, and musicians are not necessarily doing better. To understand why, it's helpful to consider, once again, cows.

There are more cows today than at any other time in history. Typically, however, the life of each individual cow is miserable, filthy, and cramped, and as soon as they've reached physical maturity, they're slaughtered. The cow's genetic information will probably persist for as long as a human's does, but is this kind of immortality desirable?

From a purely mechanistic perspective, the purpose of all life is to propagate and multiply the unique molecules we call

DNA. But purpose is not meaning. The meaning we find and create every day is a more important part of our individual lives than endless striving for replication. This is why statements like "Television programing exists to fill time between commercials" can be both literally true and patently ridiculous. If we didn't find meaning in those shows, we wouldn't tolerate the commercials. Geniuses like Pythagoras exploited this hunger for meaning to cultivate followers who would sooner perish in a fire than allow the light of the knowledge they'd accumulated to die out.

In the last century and a half, the life of a cow has changed dramatically, and so has the life of a piece of music. Music is truly everywhere. From a survival standpoint, it's thriving, like the DNA of farm animals. More music means more money for the few people who own a lot of it, but the *value* of an individual song is far less than it was even thirty years ago.

We can divide music up into three types:

> Type One: Music for narrative, which describes most music and includes songs, film scores, theatrical trailers, ballets, music for commercials, and most television background music.
> Type Two: Music for its own sake, like symphonies, chamber music, or instrumental jazz. This music exists purely for abstract pleasure.
> Type Three: Music to fill sonic space. Any type of music can be used this way, but some music is made exclusively for this purpose. This is the nondescript music in the

lobbies of corporate office buildings, music played over the phone when you're on hold, music behind a talking head on any video sharing platform. Some call this type "functional music," and there is a small but growing industry around it.

Type One music is the most lucrative per piece, the most numerous, and probably the oldest. It's also the most rigid in terms of form and formula. This is what most musicians try to make, and it's the music most people choose to listen to.

Type Two music is comparatively rare and principally consumed by the musically literate public. It has many rigid forms, but it can also be completely free of form.

Type Three music is becoming more abundant as it's become easier to produce. It's not particularly lucrative per piece and is often licensed in bulk for cheap or for free.

The music business works best for musicians when money is concentrated on the production of types One and Two. Music libraries used to specialize in Type Three music, but they now produce Type One music almost exclusively. For decades, Type Three music allowed musicians to hone their craft and make a little money in the process. But because it's easier and cheaper to create Type Three music, there's more of it, and each piece of music is worth less. The amount of music available has shot up, and so has the average quality, but compensation has gone down. A professional, non-superstar music maker used to make a fortune; now they're lucky to make a living.

AI has the potential to create way more Type Three music than any human. I believe that custom-composed music will always be the gold standard, like organic, family-farm-raised beef, but my biggest fear is that people will come to believe insipid, AI Type Three music is "good enough." Music entrepreneurs might flood the market with Type Three AI-generated music, driving down the cost while driving up the value of the music business.

So long as the value of music continues to rise, regardless of what type of music is most prevalent, the business will be profitable for non-musician administrators. Problems, inequalities, and the exploitation of creators arise in the music business when the incentives of music makers and administrators are misaligned.

Edison's phonograph and its descendants—radios, televisions, and smartphones—have become universal enhancements to human life. They operate by abstracting all information in one way or another. Whether analog or digital, there is a sense in which to these machines, everything is number. While these technologies have increased access to music and democratized its production and distribution, they also seem to have a strong bias toward leading artistic products down the path of ubiquitous mediocrity.

Maybe our technology doesn't create mediocrity but merely exposes it, but either way, we live, today, in a digital world, and, by any reckoning, there's a lot more crap out there than there used to be. Yet despite the rising tide of forgettable music, some of the legends of the twentieth and twenty-first centuries have used the new media to create transcendent works that eclipse the din of mediocrity.

BRAVE

Jon Ford is better known as JOYRYDE. He's a musician whose instrument is a laptop. He makes electronic music and has millions of fans worldwide. I don't know how much music theory he knows; we never talk about it because, when I see JOYRYDE, we're usually doing demolition.

JOYRYDE and I used to have studios next to each other in a building in Hollywood. My studio sounded fine; it wasn't great, but I got used to it. JOYRYDE built his studio into a sonic temple the likes of which I'd never seen. Then, he decided he wasn't satisfied with the sound, so he tore it all down and did it again. Once he'd built the studio into the instrument that he wanted, he began to work on his album *Brave*.

He'd had back surgery and decided to write a concept album about the experience of injury, surgery, and recovery. Writing a concept album today is almost like writing a mass or an opera: it's an established form whose golden age of popularity has passed. In the span of a few decades, this art form was born, reached its zenith, and then faded into obscurity.

Another popular musical form, the sonata—used by Bach, Mozart, Beethoven, Schubert, and even George Gershwin—remained in use for about three hundred years. The sonata is no longer "popular music," but it was able to develop for centuries and it yielded some of the most important musical masterworks in history.

By the time *Brave* debuted to critical acclaim, I had moved my studio to my home and JOYRYDE had taken over the whole 10,000-square-foot building in Hollywood. When I come back to visit or work, there's always a room under construction. There's usually a recently built studio being torn down only to be built again with a few improvements. The building is a work of art; the building is an instrument; the building is the physical manifestation of JOYRYDE's musical vision.

The sonata was actively in use for three centuries. It's like a European church: ancient, permanent, and rigid. The concept album is more like a studio in JOYRYDE's building. It's just a loose idea, a work in progress, a form that changes to suit the stories it wants to tell.

Bach and Gershwin were separated by about two hundred years, but had they somehow materialized at each other's desks, they would have recognized each other's tools. Gershwin might not have known how to prepare Bach's quill pens, and Bach might have been baffled by the precision of a manufactured pencil, but they each would have found a writing implement, manuscript paper, and a keyboard and could have gotten right to work.

Gershwin and I are separated by just eighty years, but if he were to sit at my desk, he would have no idea what he was looking at. He would find a keyboard, but mine is a MIDI controller that makes no sound until the computer is turned on and the right program is engaged. Above the controller, he'd find four flat-

COWS, DNA, AND THE MAN OF THE MILLENNIUM

screen monitors, speakers, a digital/analog converter, faders, and a six-button mouse.

If Gershwin got as far as realizing that this equipment needed to be set up and turned on, he'd never figure out how to actually do it without help and a few days of practice. My musical tools are a product of my time and the society that I live in, just as Bach's and Gershwin's were products of theirs, and just as the bone flute was a product of its maker's time and her society. It's reasonable to think that in another eighty years, music technology will be utterly incomprehensible to we early twenty-first-century humans.

In eighty years, I might sit at a composer's rig and find an empty desk, because the instrument will be on an unseen interface I don't know how to access. Guido d'Arezzo mastered prenotation choral music and invented notation to help others learn it. Hildegard von Bingen mastered the most popular musical form of her day and the notation needed to communicate and preserve it. Bach mastered his medium. Gershwin mastered his. And I've mastered mine. Every musician needs to master the medium of their time, and with every new medium, much is gained but some things are lost. Which is why a project like finishing Schubert's Unfinished Symphony with AI terrifies purists. It feels reckless, as though technology is a locomotive moving too fast, and if it continues to affect our art at this speed, it will shake loose some of what makes us human.

But technology is not a locomotive. It's more like a rollercoaster with epoch-defining peaks—like the inventions of notation and printing, or the phonograph—but it moves in a loop (to borrow science writer Jacob Ward's term) with periods of anticipation: intense periods when we feel we're losing control and long periods when we lose momentum so we can safely go round the track again. This looping pattern is found in nature, and since music is a natural phenomenon, we find it in music, too.

Five hundred and thirty million years ago, the Cambrian Explosion was followed by mass extinction. That pattern repeated five times, and we're currently living in what many scientists consider to be the planet's sixth biological epoch. We, the biota of planet Earth, have been around the rollercoaster of life five times. This cycle of creation, proliferation, and extinction is natural, observable, and universal.

Some forms change, many disappear, and only the most robust survive. If the endeavors of the human imagination, like music, art, and technology, follow any pattern, it's probably this natural, biological one. Technology is, after all, the product of living beings. It is as natural a construction as a beehive, an anthill, or a spider's web. Music has been with us for at least 60,000 years, and it will not cease to exist simply because our machines can make a lot of it. But music will, as it must, change and evolve.

My rig is a tool to solve problems quickly. It is useful in the commercial application of my musical skills, but creative problems don't always benefit from being solved quickly. In fact, solving them quickly usually leads to the imperfect solutions we've discussed so far in this book.

COWS, DNA, AND THE MAN OF THE MILLENNIUM

Creative problems don't have right or wrong answers, and they usually benefit from long deliberation. My process is fast because, like every other twenty-first century composer working in a capitalist system, I make my living not by writing music but by selling it. So, I have to be able to write it quickly and sell it often. My rig helps me create quickly.

So many AI technologies seem entertaining, disruptive, or even terrifying. Technology amuses us, but what creative people do with it amazes us. Humans, and by extension our technology, are really good at solving technical problems. Technology saves work, but creating art is not work. While the creation of art sometimes requires the artist to solve technical problems, the final product is more than the solution of those problems. The problems are part of the process and are solved in the service of drawing connections, revealing patterns, and telling stories.

Despite our technological gap, George Gershwin and I would have no trouble communicating about music. He'd have more to show me about creativity, songwriting, and orchestration than most contemporary composers. His mastery, although it seems ancient, would not have tarnished with time.

I think Gershwin would be intrigued by how quickly I can take a piece of music from inception to completion using modern tools I take for granted. If he'd had these tools, he might have written even more hit songs and iconic orchestral works. But if I wanted to show him the progress we've made in music since his death in 1937, I wouldn't show him how many tracks are on streaming servers, or how fast an artificial intelligence (or a human with a rig) can compose an insipid piece of music. I'd start by playing him *Brave*.

Initially, the sound would jar the ears of an early-twentieth-century composer of musicals, but by the time he heard the high percussion interact with the low horns of the final track—"Damn"—he'd start to understand the power of this media to tell stories. Our technology would amuse Gershwin, but he'd be amazed that we use it to achieve the same effects in recordings he achieved in staged performances. Amusement and amazement begin as the same feeling, but amazement lasts.

IV

Rondo

SAINTS, SIBYLS, SINNERS, AND SYMPHONIES

HALLELUJAH

The composer Edgard Varèse was once asked to define music. After a pensive pause, he said, "Music is organized sound."

Just as the workings of the mind cannot be explained both succinctly and meaningfully, there is no short and complete definition of the phenomenon of music. "Music is organized sound" is what philosopher Daniel Dennett would call a "deepity": it sounds profound, but it's actually so trivial that it's meaningless. "Sound" is the vibration of molecules, and "organized" is a subjective term that can mean almost anything.

In 2020, I wrote a piece called "Thought Experiment Infinity," which begins at the Big Bang and repeats silence until the end of time. I've organized all the sounds in the universe and written

UNFINISHED

Thought Experiment Infinity

all the music that has ever, or will ever, exist. Nevertheless, "music is organized sound" is about as good a definition as one could imagine. Music is no more than meaningless sounds. We tell stories with and about those sounds, and those stories give the music meaning. Meaning in music is personal and often differs from one listener to another. A piece of music can mean something totally different to its creator than it does to the audience. In fact, the creator has very little control over the meaning and interpretation of their music.

Somewhere in the world right now, a congregation of Evangelical Christians is singing Leonard Cohen's "Hallelujah." They're swaying with gently bent elbows, lost in the rapture of the song's hypnotic refrain—"Hallelujah, Hallelujah." The song tells a story about devotion and love for their imaginary creator. It tells congregants a story about themselves. The accompaniment seems inspired and religious, too. It makes use of musical tropes often found in nineteenth-century hymns. The song is modern, but it seems ancient, and that makes it feel timeless.

Somewhere in the world right now, an Evangelical Christian is listening to "Hallelujah" while he prays. And, somewhere in heaven, Leonard Cohen is laughing at him.

SAINTS, SIBYLS, SINNERS, AND SYMPHONIES

"Hallelujah" was originally one of the tracks on a 1984 album of Cohen's. After years of songwriting and months of arranging, recording, mixing, and mastering, Cohen played the album for the man who paid for it, CBS Records President Walter Yetnikoff. His response was characteristically direct. "We're not releasing it, Lenny. It's a disaster."

Yetnikoff was right. The album is a disaster. CBS Records rejected it, but in 1984, it was released by a smaller label. The album hasn't aged well. But something about "Hallelujah" caught the ears of a few important musicians.

In the 1990s, Jeff Buckley was a singer-songwriter in the New York City indie folk scene, an emotive guitar player with a sonorous, expressive, virtuosic voice. One afternoon, while he was thumbing through his friend's record collection, he found the obscure disaster of a Leonard Cohen album. He particularly liked "Hallelujah" and began performing it, usually as an encore. Audiences responded so well, he decided to record it. In 1994, ten years after Leonard Cohen's version, Buckley's haunting "Hallelujah" became an underground sensation and inspired many other covers.

It's impossible to say how many, in practice, were covers of the Leonard Cohen original and how many were covers of Jeff Buckley's version, or of Welsh musician John Cale's 1991 version, but I suspect that many performers and fans came to the song through one of these covers, as I did, and have never heard the original.

In 1999, my father, a filmmaker, was hired to direct a

documentary about the National Hockey League's Buffalo Sabres, a come-from-behind team that was having a magical season. Against all odds, they made it to the Stanley Cup finals for the first time in franchise history. As the scrappy team clawed their way through the playoffs, I was completing my senior project, working at a preschool, playing with Boomwhackers, and preparing to graduate from high school.

One of the Sabres' Stanley Cup games was scheduled to take place on the same day as my graduation, and as the director of the documentary, my father felt he had to be at the game. He could have sent someone else to cover for him, but I told him I didn't care if he saw me graduate and that he should work the game instead. He arranged for me to take a car straight from the graduation stage to the airport and fly on the client's private jet to meet him in Buffalo.*

The documentary's soundman was coming from New York City, so we shared the plane. He'd heard from my dad that I was interested in music and wanted to introduce me to some of the music he loved. He put a CD into my Discman and hit play.

As the plane took off, I listened to Jeff Buckley's cover of "Hallelujah" for the first time, and I began to cry. I realized that, while in typical teenage fashion I'd told my dad I didn't care if

---

* Documentary budgets don't usually include private jets, but the owners of the Buffalo Sabres were unusually free with their cash. As it turned out, they were also loose with their bookkeeping, and a few years later, they were found to have spent $2.3 billion of company money on personal luxuries, but that's a story for a different book.

he made it to my graduation, I was devastated he hadn't been there and felt he'd missed a piece of my life that we'd never be able to share. My dad had offered to miss the game, and would have been at my graduation if I'd insisted, but I thought it wasn't that important. I didn't realize how wrong I was until I heard that song.

In that moment, "Hallelujah" spoke to me—not the word but the sound it made in Jeff Buckley's voice. It was the sound of the anguished realization that I'd made a mistake. Buckley's virtuosity and intuitive musicality made me feel that there was a higher power above my petty emotions and that that higher power loved me and felt sorry for me.

I was in tears. I thought that the soundman was an asshole for sharing that song with me, but how could he have known how I was feeling? I was mad at my dad, and I was embarrassed to be crying next to a stranger. I felt guilty that I wasn't enjoying this free ride on a billionaire's private jet. I was suddenly overcome by the fact that, in addition to not having the most important adult in my life at my graduation, I was going to miss the parties and celebrations with the most important peers in my life in order to work as a production assistant at a Stanley Cup hockey game. I didn't even follow hockey.

It should come as no surprise that I hated the song. I hated the way I felt when I listened to it, and the intimate experience of hearing it through headphones forced me to confront those feelings head-on. For me, "Hallelujah" is forever associated with mistakes, regret, and an inability to know my own mind. Jeff Buckley's version still makes me feel like a teenager.

My first experience with "Hallelujah" was a dividing line in my life. It woke dormant feelings of insecurity and stoked a smoldering sense of loss. The song's power frightened me so much, I felt I had to understand how he had done it. To my Western mind, this meant I had to dissect it. That moment more than any other sent me down the path of becoming a professional musician.

Twenty years later, I'd accomplished that goal. I was a composer making music that made people joyful, sad, introspective, curious, excited ... I'd even written musical jokes. I'd elicited these feelings through craft, not spontaneous emotional or artistic outbursts.

While I spent my twenties and thirties reckoning with the demons Jeff Buckley's version of "Hallelujah" loosed on my psyche, the song became famous. In 2001, John Cale's earlier cover was synced to the wedding scene in the popular animated film *Shrek*. The song, despite being eighteen years old at the time, was an overnight hit. It was sung by children and their parents. It was performed at weddings in place of Mendelssohn's recessional. The song became a pop standard, a song of love, a song of devotion. The word "hallelujah" means "God be praised." But the reason Leonard Cohen is laughing at us is because we've all got it wrong.

"Hallelujah" is not a song about fathers and sons. It's not a song about weddings. It's not a song about a god, and it's definitely not appropriate for children.

It's a song about sex. When Jeff Buckley performed it live, he called it "Hallelujah to the orgasm." The Leonard Cohen album it was on, the one that the President of CBS Records thought was a disaster, is called *Various Positions*. In this song, "Hallelujah" doesn't mean "God be praised." It means "OH MY GOD!"

By the time I was commissioned to finish Schubert's Unfinished Symphony with artificial intelligence, I'd written music and performed it all over the world. I didn't think about the emotional experience I'd had on that jet after my graduation until Andy Boxall asked me, "Who put the emotion in the Unfinished Symphony, you or the AI?"

As I tried to formulate an answer to his question, I could almost hear the chorused guitar strains of Jeff Buckley's "Hallelujah" echoing through my mind. It had been twenty years since I'd first heard the song, but it was as vivid as if it were playing on a loudspeaker.

I'd spent half my life running away from the feeling the song stirred in me. I'd mastered music because I was afraid of the way music could make me feel. I enrolled in a conservatory because I was afraid of music. I became interested in the business of music because I was afraid of failing, and if I failed, I wouldn't be able to make music professionally or study it constantly. I'd be forced to listen to music like everyone else, like my nineteen-year-old self, raw and vulnerable. I was so afraid of that feeling, I had to succeed. That fear drove me from New York to Los Angeles and kept me awake all those nights at Remote Control Productions while my back ached from a car accident and my soul ached from the pain of being alone in a new city. From the moment I first heard "Hallelujah" until the moment I realized that emotion doesn't come from the music but from the listener, my every action was animated by fear disguised as obsession. What a sad way to learn an art—but that's how I learned it.

Maybe something about Jeff Buckley's voice or guitar playing invited me to feel all the feelings I'd been suppressing, but as the knowledge of the song's origin clearly demonstrates, it certainly wasn't the intent of the its composer or performer to elicit them. If a song about sex from a decades-old disaster of an album can move both Evangelical Christians and atheist high school graduates to rapturous tears, whatever meaning it contains is in the mind of the listener.

Leonard Cohen might have written "Hallelujah" because of something inside him, or someone in his life told him to write it. Who knows? Whatever the inspiration, it resulted in a work that touched millions of people. We like to think of music as a conduit from one soul to another, but the information received is often very different from the information sent.

This is less true in the craft I practice, which used to be called film scoring but is now more commonly called "media composing" or "screen composing." When creating music for media, a composer knows exactly which emotional buttons they can push to manipulate the audience's attention. Composers can shade and even shape an audience's relationship to characters and situations. This is because music has evolved over history to signal these emotions. For Western audiences, it's a rich, emotional language, codified over the last few centuries by thousands of anonymous composers and musicologists into a language of convention and cliché. We can all understand the language, but only musicians can speak it. As with any spoken or written language, music describes concepts like happiness, sadness, longing, lust, and so on, using sounds or symbols. To put this another way, these sounds and symbols are abstractions that describe emotions because we've made those associations over centuries of music-making. Just as a picture of a pipe is not a pipe, a musical phrase on its own is neither happy nor sad but a symbol whose meaning is understood in the same way by people who share a culture. The cultures of Evangelical Christianity, children who are fans of *Shrek*, and the New York City indie folk scene are very different ones. So, the same sounds and the same words can mean different things to each of them.

This type of abstraction, using symbols and sounds to represent feelings, is at the very core of music and all arts, but our representations of feelings are not inherently meaningful.

Cuneiform writing—developed in roughly the same time and place as our Mesopotamian herdswoman who invented a way to count cows—looks like the markings of a bird's feet on wet clay. The first archeologists to discover it had no idea that it was writing. But once you realize what it is, it becomes beautiful because you can see the human artifice behind it. We call the human ability to symbolically connect ideas "art," or "language," or "music." And we find that communion outside the boundaries of space and time beautiful. We also find beauty and meaning in our ability to interpret these representations of human thought and emotion.

Jeff Buckley's "Hallelujah" spoke to me. An evangelical worship leader singing the same song can send a very different message to his congregation using exactly the same sounds. Meaning in music is fungible. Without knowledge of the intention behind it, music is meaningless on its own terms. In the absence of knowledge of that intention, we infer it. When we don't know what a story is about, we make it about us.

The tools and conventions we use to create and share our feelings through music have evolved over the course of human history, becoming so elaborate and useful they are invisible. We use abstraction, not just as a tool for understanding things, but as a tool to communicate. And, sometimes, we confuse the tool with its use.

NO SAINT

Peter Abelard was a twelfth-century French monk, a philosopher, an author, a poet, and a composer who never received the honor that his lifetime of scholarship, privation, and indignity surely warranted: sainthood. He's sitting on a cloud somewhere with no wings and no harp, and he's missing a few other things too.

Over his life, Abelard grew famous for his lectures and debates. He would publicly argue with established intellectuals and show that they were wrong about the fundamentals of their philosophies. He made prominent men look silly, a dangerous pastime that bought him a reputation among the public as a formidable intellectual, and as a nuisance and agitator among the elite.

One elite scholar, sick of being made to look foolish, challenged Abelard to debate a passage of scripture. At the time, this was considered the height of intellectual activity, but to Abelard, it was just another text on which he could deploy his brilliantly polished sophistry. He responded to the challenge by insisting that the debate be held the next day on a passage of his challenger's choosing. Abelard's exposition of the passage chosen—an obscure one from Ezekiel—was so lucid that he not only won the challenge but acquired enough students to open his own school.

He wrote that his newfound fame ushered in the period of his life when he "gave free rein to his lust." He was enamored of Heloise of Argenteuil, who despite only being sixteen was already renowned for her writing and scholarship. He read her papers and fell in love with her through her work.

Abelard didn't want to marry. He wanted to dedicate his life to philosophy. But he believed a little bit of passion could give way to a lifetime of love at a comfortable distance. He fantasized that, after a tryst, he and Heloise would remain apart, pursue their intellectual passions, and write exquisite love letters. He wanted a woman in his life without having to perform the duties required of a husband. And that's pretty much what he got. Had he known how his wish would be granted, he might have chosen a more conventional path.

As a person of some renown, he had no trouble contacting

Heloise. At their first meeting, the perceptive Abelard discerned that her uncle and guardian, Fulbert, had two weaknesses: his love of money, and his passion for his niece's education.

Playing to those weaknesses, Abelard suggested to Fulbert that he should take charge of the promising young Heloise's education, and he offered to rent a room in Fulbert's house at an exorbitant price. Fulbert enthusiastically agreed and insisted that Abelard take charge of the girl's discipline, as well, instructing him to beat his niece if she was slack in her studies.

"Under the pre-text of study, we had all our time free for love," Abelard later wrote to a friend. In the same letter, he boasted that "we left no stage of love untried in our passion, and if love could find something novel or strange, we tried that, too."

During his affair with Heloise, Abelard wrote most of his surviving musical output—all love songs, some of which were still performed decades later.

Abelard and Heloise weren't careful, and everyone knew about the affair—except Fulbert. Eventually, they were caught, but by that time Heloise was pregnant and Abelard had sent her to his home in Brittany to be guarded by his family. There, she gave birth to a son whom she named Astrolabe. (Even then it was an uncommon name, but I named my youngest son Coltrane, so no judgement here.)

To keep their scandalous marriage a secret from the public, Heloise returned to live with Fulbert. But Fulbert's rage grew by the day, and eventually he hatched a plan for revenge. In the middle of a frigid night, Fulbert and several of his friends snuck into Abelard's apartment through a door left open by a servant. The men stood over Abelard as he lay sleeping in bed, and on the agreed-upon signal, they grabbed him and held him down.

Abelard awoke with a start to the sour smell of adrenaline and alcohol, unable to move. The still night air was pierced by the sound of bedclothes being torn off. His attackers held him, naked, with his legs spread wide apart. Fulbert drew a special blade, whose purpose Abelard would have recognized, and the bleariness and confusion in his otherwise brilliant eyes would have turned to terror.

Fulbert manipulated this special blade with a motion he'd practiced many times on his livestock. Abelard screamed as his body tensed, trying in vain to defend itself, but it was over in moment. The men left Abelard splayed on the bed, a freshly cut eunuch, helpless in a puddle of his own blood.

After this disfigurement, Abelard had no choice but to enter a monastery, and Heloise had no choice but to become a nun. In a horrible way, Abelard got what he wanted: a life untainted by romantic entanglements.

Abelard wrote that this violent castration was only the second worst thing that ever happened to him. We know how he felt from his letters. One letter, posthumously titled "The Calamities of Peter Abelard," details the many times he was undone by his own sinfulness, and the many men who deliberately stood in his way. In his letter he describes the worst episode in his life in great detail. It was not his castration, but an intellectual inquisition set up by rival monks.

A tribunal was called to discuss his newest book, which was then in manuscript form. It was clear to Abelard that his judges had not read the work, and he even managed to refute several of their criticisms by reading passages from the manuscript.

The sham trial came to an end when the tribunal voted that the book was indeed heretical, should not have been written without papal approval, and needed to be destroyed. They forced Abelard to burn it in their presence.

This was a public humiliation, and since no other copy of the manuscript existed, it was also a very harsh punishment.

We take for granted that a piece of work—this book, for example—is permanent once it's created. As I write this, I'm saving my work on two different hard drives in real time, one local and one off-site. I could destroy my computer and any hard copies of the book I could find without diminishing the work. But a thousand years ago, burning a few pieces of paper could destroy years of a scholar's career.

At the time, ideas were fragile. Even in written form, they were only slightly less transient than they were in the time before Theuth gave writing to the Egyptians. Ideas could be captured with the abstraction of alphabetic writing, but even in that form, they might last no more than a century or so.

Having a book copied was no small endeavor. Even someone of Peter Abelard's notoriety couldn't have his creation copied. Being forced to burn his book, to destroy the collection of abstractions he'd used to capture his thoughts, was a more profound indignity than the surprise attack that culminated in his castration.

SAINTS, SIBYLS, SINNERS, AND SYMPHONIES

In Abelard's time, powerful clergy had the ability to erase their academic rivals. We'll never know how many brilliant men and women less famous than Abelard had their life's work destroyed over similarly petty disagreements with church bureaucrats. The church fathers of the eleventh century had the power to destroy knowledge, but they also had the power to preserve it.

While Abelard was despised, and every effort was made to delete his ideas from history, one of his equally, if differently, brilliant contemporaries was endorsed by the pope. Her writings, and especially her music, were copied generation after generation until Gutenberg and d'Arezzo made it possible to print them. While Abelard tried to find his god by using logic, a practice that alienated him from his contemporaries, Hildegard von Bingen talked to her god through hallucination.

Like her contemporary Abelard, Hildegard was a brilliant interpreter of scripture and widely read, which was no small feat at a time when books were copied by hand. She viewed the word of God, which to her meant the Christian Bible, as the basis of all truth. As a result, her writing is tied in knots of mixed metaphor, imagery, and symbolism that are almost impossible to untangle. I find her writing bizarre—almost indecipherable—and I think most modern readers would feel the same way.

Her entire life, Hildegard suffered from what scholars now believe were migraines, which triggered intense, vivid visions of spirituality. At the age of forty-two, with the blessing of the pope, she began to write her visions down, and after ten agonizing years of painful hallucinations and careful writing, she published her first book.

While Abelard's relatively straightforward, logical arguments earned him opprobrium, *ad hominem* attacks, and everything short of full excommunication, Hildegard's migraine-induced visions earned her papal approval, preaching tours, and, centuries after her death, sainthood. She became the abbess of her order and was able to arrange performances of her compositions. While Abelard, like most educated people of the day, wrote music, what little survives is relatively tame, and—I'm sorry to say it, Peter—forgettable.

Despite, or maybe because of, her manic writing style, Hildegard was a wonderful composer. Her music is dramatic and eerie, and it's still performed to great effect. She was one of the most prolific composers of her time. We have seventy compositions of hers, one of which, the *Ordo Virtutum*, is the first known morality play. While it lacks the grandeur and over-the-top sensibilities of today's expressions, the *Ordo Virtutum* was in a certain sense the first Western musical, the oldest fully notated example of what would later evolve into opera.

Hildegard's audiences were nuns. Her work brought some of their inner struggles to life and gave them guidance on how to handle them—not unlike the effect contemporary pop songs have on teenagers today. In the *Ordo Virtutum*, Satan tempts the virtues by trying to appeal to their weakness, but the virtues stay strong. Singers play characters—a novel development in twelfth-century Europe. While the text seems moralizing and preachy today, the effect on an audience at the time would have been stunning.

Jeff Buckley's "Hallelujah" spoke to me because it told me a story about myself. Hildegard, too, spoke to her audience. Like every popular musician in history, she used the medium of her time to speak to the audience of her time. Her confusing voice as an author makes much more sense when she deploys it as a songwriter. She had a distinct musical sensibility and the foresight to write her music down.

In his letters, Abelard brags that a few love songs he wrote in his youth were still performed years later. Since they weren't liturgical works, he would have had no expectation that these songs would survive long beyond his death. Minstrels sang Abelard's songs on request, adding their own embellishments. Over the years, the songs evolved and changed, maybe even becoming new songs.

Hildegard's music, however, was considered part of her divine revelation and needed to be preserved exactly as she dictated it. It was transcribed using a variation of the Guidonian system.

There were probably many brilliant composers before Hildegard, but none had the right combination of skill, luck, and timing to be famous in their day and remembered in ours. Her lucky break, the break that Abelard never got, was that she was noticed and lauded by a representative of God on Earth.

In her time, Hildegard was known as the "Sybil of the Rhine," after the prophetic oracle women of Greek mythology. Her compositions are a great example of the period's music, but more importantly, they're a testament to the power of technology—in this case printing—to preserve ideas for future generations.

THE PRINCE

Carlo Gesualdo was born in Venosa, Italy, in 1566. The second son of the city's ruling family, his mother was the niece of Pope Pius IV. When he was seven years old, his mother died, and he was sent to Rome to be educated. There, he developed a passion for music that would carry him through the rest of his life. As a second son, Gesualdo expected a quiet career in the clergy that would allow him the freedom and time to compose, but the untimely death of his older brother, Luigi, made him the sole heir to the family fortune, obligating him to leave Rome, marry well, and produce a son. A marriage was arranged to Donna Maria d'Avalos, a famous beauty and the daughter of a reputable house. After their wedding, they moved to a rented apartment in the Palazzo San Severo in Naples.

Gesualdo hated Naples. He couldn't find good musicians to play his music and had no interest in court gossip. He longed for the quiet life of composition and contemplation that had been snatched from him. He found no solace in his marriage and paid only scant attention to his beautiful wife. He would probably have preferred the solitary life of a monk.

The popular music of the day was the madrigal: a secular song written for a small group of singers, sometimes with instrumental accompaniment. Madrigals are usually modal, meaning the music remains more or less within one key. They're a bit like pop songs in that they tell a story. Each singer performs a poem or a lament as a single character. Gesualdo was a master of the style, and his work might have been remembered, at least by scholars, along with that of his contemporaries, even if the macabre details of his life hadn't stained his legacy with blood.

Although her husband was cold and distant, Gesualdo's wife, Maria, seemed to enjoy life in Naples and developed a close friendship with Duke Fabrizio Carafa, a highborn playboy as renowned for his good looks as she was for her beauty. Years of Gesualdo's indifference toward his wife, and later their infant son, drove Maria into the arms of her handsome young friend. The affair went on for months, possibly years, before Gesualdo got suspicious.

On the morning of October 16, 1590, Gesualdo announced that he was going hunting and would not return until late in the evening, having conspired with a servant to leave the front door unlocked so that he could sneak back in undetected.

After a few hours, Gesualdo stalked silently into his own home with a trusted friend. Blades drawn, they burst into the marital chamber to find Maria naked and her lover, inexplicably, wearing her nightgown. The accomplice ran the adulterous Duke Fabrizio Carafa through with his rapier, while Gesualdo stabbed his wife with a dagger.

As he crossed the threshold of the bedchamber, Gesualdo paused and said to his friend, "I don't believe she's really dead." He rushed back into the room in a renewed fit of rage and stabbed his wife's mangled corpse until he exhausted himself.

Up to this point, the story of Maria's murder is factual as reported in court documents. What happened after Gesualdo re-entered the room, however, has become a dark legend. After he tired of maiming his wife's corpse, Gesualdo threw the bodies of the mangled lovers into the street to be further defiled by rodents. A strange and demented passing monk was seen interfering with the corpses before the authorities came to collect them.

And then there was the child.

Unsure that the boy was his, Gesualdo decided to murder his infant son so he wouldn't grow up to seek revenge. He suspended the baby from a banister and played lullabies to him on his lute until he died.

Before Gesualdo could be arrested for questioning, he fled to his ancestral home in Venosa, barricaded himself in his castle, and ordered his servants to cut down the forest surrounding his lands so that he could see his enemies approaching.

He was a nobleman, and what he'd done was, unbelievably, lawful by the standards of the day, since he'd caught the lovers *in flagrante delicto*. The real danger was from Maria's relatives seeking a vendetta. But they never came.

After the murder, Gesualdo's music began to change. He remarried—what a lucky lady!—and moved to Ferrara, a renowned musical city that was home to a trio of virtuoso singers. He wrote music for them that pushed the boundaries of the madrigal style. The librettos, which he likely wrote himself, were dark and disturbing. Some said he was possessed by a demon. His most famous piece, written in this later period, was called "Moro Lasso"—*Alas, I Die*. Here is an English translation of the text:

> I die, alas, in my suffering,
> And she who could give me life,
> Alas, kills me and will not help me.
> O sorrowful fate,
> She who could give me life,
> Alas, gives me death.

What sets "Moro Lasso" apart as a composition is not only its terrible history but Gesualdo's use of chromaticism. He used notes outside the keys in the way an edgy twentieth-century composer would. Gesualdo's later madrigals are written in a harmonic language that was not heard again for three hundred years. He was so far ahead of his time, it's like finding an early draft of Michael Jackson's "Thriller" in the papers of J. S. Bach.

These works were not popular in his lifetime, but his later madrigals experienced a resurgence in the twentieth century, kindled by fascination with the bizarre narrative of his life, and stoked by his sense of harmony, which is adventurous even by modern standards. The juxtaposition of his musical sensitivity and innovation with his social misanthropy and savagery stand out as an incongruity in history, too fascinating to ignore.

We may never have heard "Moro Lasso" were it not for the tragic fate of Maria d'Avalos and her lover; but their murders would have been forgotten were it not for the eerily dark, strangely enlightened music of the man who committed them.

Elsewhere in sixteenth-century Italy, opera was beginning to take shape. Gesualdo's contemporary, Claudio Monteverdi, had begun to experiment with bigger ensembles and singers playing individual characters. Hildegard had already done this in the morality plays she wrote for her nuns, but Monteverdi was telling larger stories for a broader audience. To keep his audience engaged, he used a familiar, relatively simple harmonic language.

Gesualdo left every aspect of the medieval madrigal unchanged except the harmony, which he radically modernized. Monteverdi radically modernized everything about the madrigal but made only modest changes to the harmony. His music was a permanent part of the canon in his lifetime and is regularly performed today. Monteverdi was able to control novelty in a way that allowed his audiences to be entertained and amazed but not utterly confused—surprised, but not too surprised.

Centuries later, another composer with a complicated personal history combined and enhanced the narrative techniques of Monteverdi and the harmonic techniques of Gesualdo, leading to the golden age of opera.

MEYERBEER'S PROTÉGÉ

The nineteenth-century composer Richard Wagner alienated almost everyone he ever met, but he changed music and theater forever.

In Wagner's era, operas were staged in well-lit concert halls with the orchestra visible between the audience and the stage. Wagner thought this was crude, cartoonish, not to be taken seriously. He thought it led to the stagnation of the genre as light entertainment, and that it could be more than that. He thought that if it were more immersive, opera could move people.

He imagined a staging in which the orchestra was hidden in a pit, invisible to the audience, and envisioned lavish sets with moving parts. He imagined actors who inhabited the role instead of merely singing the music. He wanted actors to ignore the audience, allowing them to become immersed in the story. He wanted smoke, curtains covering set changes, and a lit stage, while the audience sat in darkness. In other words, Wagner imagined what we now think of as a staged performance.

Wagner's pioneering innovations are still part of my job as a media composer, a century and a half later. Wagner also conceived of music as subordinate to story, the way media music is used today. He identified his characters with recurring musical themes, called *leitmotifs*, which media composers still do: think of Darth Vader's "Imperial March" or Indiana Jones's theme music. Wagner used previously unimagined orchestral textures to evoke other worlds. He mixed, matched, and violated orchestral conventions and musical cliches to suggest complicated emotions and enhance the subtext of an actor's performance.

These concepts were floating around in the artistic ether of the nineteenth century, but Wagner pulled them together. Once he got the mixture right, the effect on the audience was immediate and intense.

He spent his life creating what he called *Gesamkuntswerk*, a "total work of art," employing all the artistic disciplines. He was obsessed with every detail of his creation, and his comprehensive approach is still the foundation of modern entertainment.

If I'm scoring a movie, I work on the music, the set designer works on the look of the interiors, the costume designer works on the clothes—but the director is responsible for the total finished product and is expected to have a creative voice in every aspect of the production. This vision began with Wagner, who might have been the most important single person in the performing arts of the last two hundred years.

But you can't mention Wagner without talking about Hitler.

In 1933, fifty years after Wagner's death, Adolf Hitler was his biggest fan. Hitler insisted that Wagner's music open his Nuremberg rallies. He tried to institute a compulsory annual pilgrimage to the Bayreuth Festspielhaus, a customized theater that was, and still is, dedicated to performing Wagner's work. To Hitler's chagrin, his followers were far less passionate about Wagner than he was.

Wagner spent his career under royal patronage and considered himself anything but the "common man" to whom Hitler so successfully appealed. He would probably have hated Hitler, but they had one big thing in common: they were both rabidly, vocally antisemitic.

While Wagner made a fortune and achieved mythical status near the end of his career, for the first few decades of his life, he was continuously in debt. He held several mid-level musical posts in major European cities, but he routinely fled to avoid creditors. He became a member of the royal court at Dresden and achieved early success there with his first opera, *Rienzi*. But when he participated in a socialist uprising, he became an official pariah and was forced to flee the city.

In exile, he wrote essays voluminously, and some of his writing from that period is still interesting and relevant. However, his most infamous essay, "Das Judenthum in der Musik"—"Jewishness in Music"—published under a pseudonym in in 1850, lays out the reasons for his antisemitism. This is his argument in a nutshell:

1. According to Wagner, Europeans instinctively hate Jews for the following reasons:
    A. Jews don't look like Europeans.
    B. Jews speak with weird accents.
    C. Jews also sing, write, and play music with weird accents.
2. Jews control the world.
3. Jews control the arts.

These are not really arguments, and I won't waste space discussing their merit. Wagner pontificates on his idea that Jews speak and play music with an accent, and he specifically calls out the composer Felix Mendelssohn, a baptized and practicing Lutheran, whose paternal grandfather, Moses Mendelssohn, was the preeminent Jewish philosopher of his day.

Mendelssohn was only four years older than Wagner, but the first part of Wagner's career was spent in Mendelssohn's shadow. Before Wagner had even touched an instrument, the young Mendelssohn was a featured soloist at private concerts for European nobility. One of the most famous poets and polymaths in history, Johann Wolfgang von Goethe, declared Felix Mendelssohn the greatest prodigy the world had ever seen. Goethe, who had heard young Mozart perform and rejected a dedication of songs from Franz Schubert, knew some of the best musicians in history and was not generous with his praise. But he was effusive about Mendelssohn.

In 1835, Mendelssohn was named *Kapellmeister*—musical director—of the orchestra in Wagner's hometown, Leipzig. Wagner submitted the score to his Symphony in C Major to be considered for performance. Mendelssohn not only didn't program it, he lost the manuscript. He *did* program a work by an almost forgotten Viennese composer, Franz Schubert, instead. Were it not for Mendelssohn's fresh new interpretations, Schubert's work might have been relegated to academia.

In 1840, the King of Prussia established a music school in Berlin, part of an effort to turn the city into the cultural capital of Europe. Wagner desperately wanted to become the head of this school, but the king had never heard of him. He instead appointed the best composer of the day, Felix Mendelssohn, leading to the most productive period of Mendelssohn's career.

Among Mendelssohn's compositions was a march that is still regularly performed at the end of weddings today, part of his incidental music for Shakespeare's *A Midsummer Night's Dream*. In a piece of cosmic irony, Wagner's most widely known piece of music is played at weddings, too. The melody most people know as "Here Comes the Bride" is from his opera *Lohengrin*.

Tragically, in 1847, Mendelssohn died of a stroke at the age of thirty-eight. It's safe to say that his best musical years would have been ahead of him. Wagner waited until 1850, three years after Mendelssohn's untimely death, to offer his scathing critique of the "Jewishness" of the great composer's work.

Had Mendelssohn lived, we might never have heard of Wagner. He might have toiled away in obscurity as the second-best German composer of the nineteenth century. But Wagner enjoyed longevity and found a voice for himself in the vacuum left by his rival.

On March 10, 1846, the Bavarian king Maximillian II died unexpectedly, elevating his eighteen-year-old son, Ludwig II, to the throne. Like a teenager who'd discovered an indie band, Ludwig was obsessed with Wagner's operas. He was determined to be a great patron of the arts and believed that Wagner could become the most powerful voice in modern opera if he just had a little help. (To his credit, the king was right.) One of his first royal acts was to find the exiled Wagner, pardon him for his crimes against the monarchy, and invite him to Munich.

Wagner's operas were the most elaborately staged productions in history. They were transporting, energizing, perhaps even terrifying. And they required new technology in the form of a specially built theater, which King Ludwig II commissioned in Bayreuth. In the early days of the Bayreuth theater, the production tricks and rousing, loud music worked audiences into a rapturous frenzy, using some of the same techniques we still use in theatrical trailers today. In this frenzied state, audiences were served stories of German nationalism.

For an audience steeped in the tradition of pre-Wagnerian opera, this was an enhancement of the art form, and it made the message seem incredibly important, which I think is why Hitler loved it so much.

The emotion in Wagner's music came not from the notes themselves, but from the entire production and the narrative it depicted. Hitler liked classical music and opera, and he knew its traditions. It's been well-documented that Hitler also loved German nationalism. To a less refined audience of Nazis in 1933, Wagnerian spectacle was just normal theater. In fact, when they consumed a narrative of a German nationalism they already fervently believed in, delivered in a medium that was totally familiar and a bit old-fashioned, many of them found it boring, even a bit moralizing and preachy.

Fifty years after his death, Wagner's operas had become as hackneyed as the ones he'd spent his life trying to reform. For some audiences, these operas seemed even more silly because they took themselves so seriously.

Wagner's techniques of character themes, elaborate staging, realistic acting, and music that existed to serve the story remained in use after his death. But if the Nazis hadn't revived his music and brought it to worldwide attention, it's not clear that his personality would have been as attached to those techniques as it is.

Wagner was very popular in his day, especially toward the end of his life, but equally popular composers have been forgotten. Composers tend to be remembered when they're associated with a major world event or horrible crime. We use music to commemorate major historical events and people just as our ancestors used music to tell the story of their tribe.

The lasting fascination with his life and work might be due to his posthumous association with the Nazis, but either way, Wagner was a genius. Even a genius gets his start somewhere, and Wagner got his with help from a no less brilliant but nearly forgotten contemporary.

Wagner's first opera, *Rienzi*, wasn't programmed at the Dresden Court Theater because his genius was recognized. It was programmed because the most prominent composer of the day, Giacomo Meyerbeer, shepherded the opera into the company and all but insisted they perform it.

Meyerbeer came out of the tradition of the First Viennese School of classical composers. He was taught by Antonio Salieri, who taught Beethoven and Schubert (and who, I repeat, did not kill Mozart). In 1840, Meyerbeer was the most famous composer in the world and could probably have made any opera house produce anything if he agreed to let them stage one of his operas as well. His name alone guaranteed sold-out attendances.

As a young man, Wagner reached out to Meyerbeer with

a painfully effusive and groveling letter that all but begged for his help. Meyerbeer may have been one of the only people to recognize young Wagner's talent, and he wrote letters of introduction to some of the most prominent musicians in Europe, securing his first performance.

Why has a composer of Meyerbeer's status been totally forgotten? He's never had a real evangelist—not one with the reach of Hitler, anyway. Meyerbeer's work was banned in Germany in the mid-twentieth century because—you guessed it—he was Jewish.

His style of Grand Opera employed many of the same techniques Wagner later refined. Wagner didn't so much invent his opera style out of whole cloth as he adjusted and embellished the style of his mentor Meyerbeer. For obvious reasons, Meyerbeer does not appear in "Jewishness in Music." Wagner owed his career to this Jewish maestro, and his posterity to Hitler.

What does this have to do with the use of artificial intelligence to make art? Part of the answer is in a short story I loved as a child.

THE QUIXOTE

When I was in high school, I was obsessed with a short story collection by Jorge Louis Borges titled *Labyrinths*. I've since read it many times, and I always find something new in it.

One of Borges's stories, "Pierre Menard, Author of the Quixote" is about a man who, in the early twentieth century, sets out to write the sixteenth-century classic *Don Quixote*. He doesn't want to copy it, and he hasn't read Cervantes. He wants to write, from scratch, a work that already exists.

Pierre Menard quickly realizes that he must learn sixteenth-century Spanish and must live as close as possible to the way the book's author, Miguel De Cervantes, lived. The story masterfully walks us through the details of this project. Pierre Menard eventually succeeds in writing a chapter or so of *The Quixote*, which is more or less like the original.

An accomplishment, maybe...but what's the point?

Why isn't his accomplishment important? It should be as impressive a feat as it was for Cervantes, right? Repeating an artistic act demonstrates that skill in itself is not that interesting. Skill says something about the person who acquired it, but it doesn't tell a story. Skill alone can't move an audience.

When we watch a performance, we want the performer to tell us something about ourselves. I mean this in the personal sense, the way Leonard Cohen's songwriting and Jeff Buckley's singing moved me as deeply as it can move a person of faith. I mean it in the national sense, the way Wagner spoke to the budding nation of Germany and told them who they were. I mean it in the universal sense, the way Pythagoras and other religious geniuses remind us of humanity's special, privileged place in creation. All these performers used their skills not to glorify themselves but to tell us about who we are.

We want to hear just the right amount about ourselves. Too little, and the work is vapid; too much, and the work is didactic.

Because taste and human knowledge are fluid over generations, the perfect balance in one generation may be too much or too little in another.

In the era of oral transmission, stories could change from one generation to the next. Art was a dynamic, living thing. Today, as Tiokasin Ghosthorse said, art has been "nounified" to death. Any art object—a painting, a photograph, or a recorded piece of music—is static. To appreciate a work from another time requires a knowledge of the time and place of its creation. Without that knowledge, the work can only be interpreted through the distorted lens of the viewer's biases and assumptions. Work that was cutting-edge in one time might seem trite or make no sense in another.

Hildegard's nuns were probably impressed with her musical skill, but what spoke to them in her music was the story she told about them. Abelard's music was clever, and his prose was brilliant, but Hildegard's work gave her medieval audience what they wanted: to feel the ecstasy of the glory of their creator. Her music left audiences surprised, but not too surprised. Abelard simply gave his audiences a hard and honest look at their beliefs.

Abelard got castrated, and Hildegard got sainted.

Monteverdi gave his audiences complex stories they already knew, but he added the heightened elements of operatic style, and they loved it. Gesualdo showed people that a technical aspect of music—harmony—could be stretched way past the conventional breaking point and still be beautiful, but that was an idea and not a story; only composition students like me truly care.

SAINTS, SIBYLS, SINNERS, AND SYMPHONIES

Why does this music sound the way it does, and what does that sound mean for those who make it? Those who hear it are part of the ecosystem that makes music possible. Music is not a product but a process. It is not simply "organized sound" but sound organized in a way that conveys meaning to the listener. The difference is subtle, but without an audience, music is just noise. It becomes art when someone hears it and tries to make sense of it.

Given the time and resources, anyone could have done what Pierre Menard did. His accomplishment is amusing, but it's not amazing. Why is Cervantes's *Don Quixote* a masterwork while Menard's is, at best, a curiosity? "Music is the search for new sounds" is a passable explanation, but it doesn't really get at what music is. Music is not a noun—it's a verb, a living thing that constantly changes.

What we find interesting in music is controlled novelty, and the art lies in both the novelty and the control. Musicians study for years to learn how to balance these two elements. Achieving controlled novelty is more difficult than its stated simplicity might suggest. Even the most talented musicians who study fervently for years often get it wrong.

Conservatories have large buildings full of practice rooms where musicians spend untold hours mastering their instruments. For four years, while I was in school, I almost lived in a practice room. On a busy day, I'd practice for two hours; on a normal day, I'd practice for five hours; and on a good day, I'd practice for twelve hours. My playing was initially so mediocre that I almost wasn't admitted to a conservatory, but by the time I left, I was one of the best in my class.

Before I arrived at my music school audition, I had exhausted the limits of my talent, and what musical knowledge, prowess, or skill I've developed since then could be acquired by anyone who had the opportunity and the drive to practice as hard, and as much, as I did. I've acquired skill, but that's not what makes me a good musician.

Musicians all start out like Pierre Menard. We try to re-create and reproduce the works of the past, though perhaps not quite as literally. But learning the craft is just the beginning of a musical journey. The art of music is knowing which parts of the tradition are still important and which need to be discarded or revised.

FALSE HOPE

When I was a music student, I didn't listen to Hildegard von Bingen's inspiring music, or Gesualdo's terrifying music, or Wagner's triumphant music. I listened to swingin', hip, complicated, esoteric, downtown jazz. Like Pierre Menard, who lived like Cervantes and spoke only Spanish, I talked, acted, and lived like the people who made the music I loved. The music I listened to spoke to me about love and ascetic devotion to an art form.

One of the composers who told me a story about myself was the jazz great Elmo Hope. Elmo Hope's music was largely forgotten after his death, overshadowed by the music

SAINTS, SIBYLS, SINNERS, AND SYMPHONIES

of Thelonious Monk, Bud Powell, and the many other notable bandleaders of the 1950s and '60s. Today, only the dedicated few who wouldn't blush at being called jazz superfans know about Hope. His compositions are a permanent but minor part of the jazz canon.

In 2004, jazz guitar legend Kurt Rosenwinkel played a weekly concert at a late-night, smoke-filled club called Small's in New York's West Village. My conservatory classmates and I never missed it, and Rosenwinkel often played a few of Elmo Hope's tunes in his set. One student and I discussed how hip it was that Rosenwinkel was reviving the music of this previously unknown composer.

So, who was Elmo Hope? He played on a few recordings, though not as many as the jazz stars of his day. I was a dedicated student of jazz, a jazz superfan, yet I knew almost nothing about him. I had just enough information to get all the details wrong.

To me, Elmo Hope was a man of uncompromising artistic integrity. He was outside "the scene," but his music was so good that fifty years later, it's still performed. It survived him and became an eternal legacy to a life lived in pursuit of artistic perfection, a legacy Kurt Rosenwinkel inherited and I hoped to inherit as well.

Elmo Hope decided to forego fame for truth, and what is more appealing to an obsessed artistic youth than commitment to unattainable austerity?

My connection with Hope's music made me feel bohemian, even though I'm from the suburbs. It made me feel like an expert, even though I was a student. And it made me feel my artistic life might have a purpose, if I could just stay true to my vision, as Elmo had.

It wasn't until I began researching this book that I realized the Elmo Hope of my imagination was not the Elmo Hope of history.

The historical Elmo Hope was a jazz pianist and composer who was active in New York City in the 1940s and '50s. He played on the 1953 album *New Faces, New Sounds*, which featured Clifford Brown and Lou Donaldson and is considered one of the first examples of the hard-bop sound that would dominate the next decade. Elmo wasn't just part of the scene; he was at its vanguard.

However, Hope was plagued by heroin addiction, and, because of a criminal conviction, he lost his cabaret card. In New York at that time, a cabaret card was a license to perform. Losing it meant Hope could no longer perform within the city limits. He'd lost his prominent place in jazz history not through some herculean feat of uncompromising austerity, but because of a legal issue. He'd been a big part of "the scene," but his addiction got him run out of town.

Even as I write this, the historical Elmo Hope and the one I invented so many years ago seem like two different people. Indeed, they are, because one of them is a figment of my imagination. I knew a few scattered details about Elmo Hope's life and stitched them into a story that said more about me than about him. The story drew me to his music and encouraged me to interpret it as though it were rebellious and iconoclastic—although really, it was fairly typical, even prototypical, for the period.

The music of Leonard Cohen, Hildegard, Abelard, Gesualdo, Wagner, and Elmo Hope caught my attention, but the emotional bond of imagined kinship or morbid fascination kept me engaged with them and drew me further into their worlds.

I've told the stories of these composers, who are separated by nearly a thousand years, to illustrate something that is second nature to promoters, politicians, record executives and advertisers: context matters.

The context in which we listen to music dictates the way we form an emotional bond with it. We can form a bond with the idea of a person, historical or imagined. Richard Wagner's music was not performed in Israel until the year 2000 because, for all his musical innovations, his posthumous association with the Nazis and his fallacious, ridiculous, antisemitic writings made his person a painful reminder of the worst atrocity of the twentieth century.

Leonard Cohen's song about sex, put in the context of Shrek's animated wedding, made it an instant classic among children and the religious. Abelard's forgettable music survives because of the significance of his other work, and his famously tragic love affair. Hildegard's music survives because of her religion and the technological advances of her day. Meyerbeer's music, although produced on the cusp of modernity with far more technological advantages than Hildegard had, almost didn't survive because of his ethnicity. Gesualdo's music lives on as a reminder of the brutal murder that drove its perpetrator mad to the point of chromaticism. To me, possibly to me alone, Elmo Hope's music represents the sacrifice of earthly fame to the cause of artistic enlightenment.

Emotional bonds allow this music to live on, and an AI composer would have to replicate those bonds to compete with an accidental pop star, an antisemitic genius, a Jewish genius, a eunuch, a zealot, an imaginary iconoclast, or a murderous medieval prince.

Can artificial intelligence make music in a context that will allow us to form an emotional connection with it? Can it use our abstraction of sound in a way we find meaningful? Maybe. But what would be the point?

We can already make completely AI-created music. Maybe someday AI will be able to write a symphony, orchestrate it, print it, play it, mix it, master it, and do all the press around it. But why? This would be an impressive show of skill, and skill can amuse us, but only meaning can amaze us.

Will a piece of AI music "mean" something someday? Or will AI music forever be like Pierre Menard's *Quixote*, technically an accomplishment, but a meaningless, pointless one?

CODA

GODS

As far back as recorded history goes, humans have ascribed the events of the observable world to gods. But gods, while they might get you sainted or castrated, don't get results. Science, on the other hand, continues to produce answers to previously unanswerable questions. More importantly, science continues to make new questions possible.

While science is measurably more reliable than religion at explaining the universe and discovering practical, useful information, both approaches have blind spots. The blind spots in religion are obvious. A non-religious person sees them in every religion. Religious people see them in every religion but their own.

The blind spots in science are much more subtle, far more pernicious, and may be impossible to reconcile. A dogmatic belief that science will one day reveal a universal set of laws has animated the work of geniuses like Albert Einstein, Isaac Newton, and Pythagoras. Yet at the moment, there's no evidence that such a set of truly universal laws exists, and some evidence that they do not—at least, there's some evidence we're looking for these laws in the wrong way.

The numerical hypothesis of existence—Pythagoras's belief that "everything is number," that everything is computable—is still a prevailing secular belief. But it's only one in a long line of theories that, while fruitful, helpful, and even essential, are not necessarily true.

Ideas as old as the numerical hypothesis of existence are like the sixty-second division on the face of a clock. They've become so ingrained in our minds and culture that we no longer look at them critically. The numerical hypothesis of existence is not a universal law. It's a hypothesis.

And it's wrong.

In 1814, eight years before Schubert began to write but not finish his eighth symphony, the French mathematician Pierre-Simon Laplace was already speculating, in a roundabout way, that it might be possible to finish it using AI. He thought an "intellect"—referred to today as "Laplace's Demon"—would someday be able to know and predict everything, and that my exploits and yours would be fully known to it.

Laplace imagined a machine that would be able to tell the future or peer into the past with absolute certainty. "We may regard the present state of the Universe as the effect of its past and the cause of its future," he wrote at the beginning of his essay "A Philosophical Essay on Probabilities." He went on: "An intellect, which at a certain moment would know all forces that set nature in motion and all positions of all items of which nature is composed, if this intellect were also vast enough to submit these data to analysis, would embrace in a single formula the movements of the greatest bodies of the Universe and those of the tiniest atom: for such an intellect nothing would be uncertain and the future, like the past, would be present before its eyes."

Laplace is saying that if any intelligence, even an artificial one, knew the location and momentum of every particle in the universe, it could use the Newtonian equations of motion to predict the future positions of those particles with absolute certainty.

Of course, this is pure deductive reasoning, extrapolating future results from past actions. This type of calculation is computable. Laplace's Demon could know how particles would behave if it could learn how they had behaved in the past. Knowledge of the position and momentum of every particle in the universe should yield absolute knowledge of the physical state of the entire universe's future.

Is this knowledge possible for a sophisticated AI? Computers grow more powerful every day. Will they, someday soon, be powerful enough to become the "vast intellect" Laplace could only imagine? Can we create an omnipotent AI god? Since the industrial age, it's always seemed to be about ten years away.

In Laplace's view, to be omnipotent, an entity would have to know the "positions of all items of which nature is composed." "Items" is the tricky word here. Laplace didn't know about the very real but strange items we know about today. He didn't know about subatomic particles and their seemingly random and probabilistic behavior. Nor did he know about the Heisenberg Uncertainty Principle—that no matter how vast intelligence is, it can't know both the position and momentum of a given subatomic particle.

Laplace's Demon is the ultimate extension of Pythagoras's theory that "everything is number." In 1814, it seemed that could be true, but today, given what we know about basic quantum physics (if anything about quantum physics can be called "basic"), the thought experiment has become an illustration of the absurdity of the numerical hypothesis of existence.

In defiance of Pythagoras and some the smartest people in the world, I will say emphatically that everything is *not* number. Some things cannot be represented by numbers. The base level of reality for a computer is a number, so some things cannot, in principle, be represented by a computer.

Some things are not computable. Is human consciousness one of those things?

In the last three hundred years, all human composers combined have written a total of a few thousand symphonies. It's hard to find an exact number, but it's in the ballpark of two or three thousand. I'm proud of the fact that, in 2019, I wrote half of one. I consider the work I composed with AI to finish Schubert's Eighth my own First Symphony. And I consider this book my Second Symphony. Both projects are unconventional. Symphony No. 2 isn't even music, but conventions, musical or otherwise, evolve with technology.

My name appears at the top right-hand corner on the final

CODA

two movements of Schubert's Unfinished Symphony, finished with artificial intelligence. The piece has been performed around the world and the reviews have been predictably mixed. Reviews of Beethoven's symphonies were mixed, too. I've lost no sleep over the critiques.... Okay, that's a lie. I've lost countless hours of sleep fretting over my critics, but please don't tell them, and permit me my feigned stoicism.

Some people loved the piece. Some said it wasn't "Schuberty" enough. Some said it was a triumph of technology. But no one denied that it was a piece of music. It was a symphony. However anyone feels about its artistic merits or authenticity, the fact is that a few tenths of a percent of our symphonic canon has now been composed in collaboration with artificial intelligence.

I put the decision of which parts of Schubert's work were important and should be retained, and which parts could be ignored, into the hands of an AI. I interpreted its results and was the filter. Some decisions in a few tenths of a percent of the symphonic canon were not made by a human being. Maybe this number will grow in the future, but is that really anything new?

A mathematical formula—an algorithm—determined several aspects of the two movements I finished with artificial intelligence. Music has been shaped by formulas for all of its history. These forms and formulas are far simpler than the algorithms that comprise an AI composer, but they are conceptually identical. They are abstract representations of ideas too big to describe both succinctly and meaningfully.

Artists find new patterns in nature, and scholars find patterns within the arts. Sonata form evolved to describe the music people were already writing.

Trailer music was not conceived before there were theatrical trailers. Its three-act structure exists because those kinds of tracks were being used by trailer editors who, in some cases, cut together parts of different songs to achieve that structure, and composers used the formula to respond to the demand. The form of a pop song evolved over a few decades, and we have recorded evidence of that evolution. The form, in George Gershwin's time, was one verse, and then a two or four-part chorus repeated over and over. Today it's a repeated short verse, a repeated chorus, and a bridge in a prescribed order.

Our music is evolving. In a hundred or a thousand years, a musicologist will impose a period on all the music that is current today. We experience an endless library of music in many different styles and genres, but someday, someone will find a few aspects that make the music of our time identifiable and unique. They'll extract formulas we can't see to describe all of twenty-first century music. Maybe melodies created by AI will have a certain characteristic that musicians in the future will be able to identify with ease, the same way a human can pick out the difference between Mozart and George Gershwin.

Artificial intelligence is just part of our human creative process. We invented it, like we invented every other tool, to create, consume, and commercialize our arts. Now we use it to make music. We use it to search for new sounds that can help us make new meaning. What could possibly be more human?

CODA

When a song was written on a piece of paper, who performed it was unimportant. When it was impossible to preserve a performance, the song was the notes and the melody. We think of one artist playing a song made famous by another artist as a "cover," but before recording, all songs were covers, and even widely known performers were unable to preserve their art.

Today, we think of the master recording as the song, and sheet music has become ephemera that is often discarded after the recording session—if the song was even written down in the first place.

Because the symphony is an art form that reached the height of popularity before the age of recording, it still adheres to the convention of being attributed to the composer. But a symphony could just as easily be associated with the orchestra or conductor who performs it. In the case of famous conductors and soloists, the performer is sometimes more important than the composer. Most Yo-Yo Ma fans will be happy to go to a concert to hear him play anything at all. They're there for him, not the repertoire. I wrote earlier that composers have always been servants of the performers, who are necessary for the music to be heard. Since technology has allowed the performer's art to live beyond their lifetime and geography, performers have eclipsed composers even in posterity.

The convention of the composer's name at the top of the page leads to a fallacy that composers are solely responsible for every note and gesture. The blueprint of a symphony, the written score, has passed through the hands of many skilled craftsmen before it gets to a concert or recording stage. Each of these craftsmen has added something to the finished product. That's why an artificial intelligence needs human help to finish Schubert's Unfinished Symphony. Music is a process.

Non-musicians think of a symphony as something you hear, and they consider the score an abstraction. To me, the sound is the abstraction, and the symphony is tangible—something I can hold, see, and read.

A symphony is a collection of abstract ideas in abstract notation developed in an imperfect system over a thousand years of practical use. And a symphony is symbols on a page that represent ideas and instructions for how to create sounds. These symbols, which have evolved since the time of Guido d'Arezzo, are expressed in notation, and audiences experience the sounds indicated by that notation as a symphony. The product is what you hear, but the symphony is a living process.

I didn't know I thought about music this way until I had to explain it to a machine.

Working with artificial intelligence taught me to question the assumptions I make when thinking about my own craft. This book is the result of some of that introspection. It's an account of my small revolution, offered in the hope that it may help spark yours.

It is the job of every artist in the age of artificial intelligence to think about what we know and learn about how we think. Our job has always been to guide audiences to rethink what happens inside their minds, to tell them a story about themselves, to create small, and sometimes large, revolutions.

CODA

This has always been the artist's job. And our job is never more necessary than in times of historical change. Technology has given us access to powers so great that we'll expose more truth about the human mind, consciousness, and soul than any generation before us.

We stand on the shoulders of giants like the maker of the bone flute, the anonymous Mesopotamian who invented base-sixty math, Pythagoras, Guido d'Arezzo, Hildegard von Bingen, Abelard, Gutenberg, Schubert, Meyerbeer, Wagner, Turing, and the thousands of brilliant scientists working on artificial intelligence right now. They have given us the tools to make art that is more powerful, more beautiful, and more profound than anything we can imagine.

Artificial intelligence is nothing less, and nothing more, than a prosthetic for the human mind. It will enhance art the way writing enhanced memory, printing enhanced literature, and recording enhanced music. Artificial intelligence is a printing press, and we're in the age of the Gutenberg Bible when we ask this powerful tool to give us more of what we already know. Soon we'll learn to ask it for new things, and use them to bring new, currently unthinkable ideas forward.

Whatever new technologies may emerge to change the course of music history, the symphony of human meaning, storytelling, and artistic expression will always be unfinished.

ACKNOWLEDGMENTS

My two greatest fears are that I'm going to leave someone out of these Acknowledgments, and that I'm going to spell someone's name wrong. I've almost certainly done both; please forgive me. I generally didn't thank you here if you're mentioned in the book.

Of course, my mother and father, Esmeralda Santiago and Frank Cantor, are responsible for my very existence, so "thank you" probably isn't enough. Thank you to my brothers and sisters Ila Cantor, River Rudl, and Sarah Cantor, and my nieces and nephews; in that list are three musicians who are better than me.

Bob Hansmann taught me how to play guitar. Doug Munro of Purchase College was the first person outside of my family to believe that I could become a professional musician.

Peter Rubie, my agent, believed in this book more than anyone on the planet including me. Without him I would have given up many years ago. Chris Chappell believed in this book enough to acquire it, edit it, and shepherd it to completion.

Professor Rebecca Fiebrink showed me what music technology is and discussed the ideas in the book with me at great length over many years. She and her wife Arianne

Alexander (who also played principal viola in the premiere of the Unfinished Symphony, Finished with AI), have hosted me at their home in London too many times to count. I love them and their two wonderful children.

Professor Daniel Murfet and I had many conversations over many years about the content of this book, and his feedback was invaluable.

Oren Neiman has been a close friend for decades, and he's the one I went to all those Kurt Rosenwinkel concerts with. Thanks to him, his wife Katie Wasserman, and their children.

Cliff Fluet is my advisor, my mentor, my friend, and the godfather of music technology. He and I have discussed the ideas in this book on at least three continents, but most productively in the confines of the Ivy.

Eric Hogensen, Sanny Rider, Drew Thurlow, Geneviève Gros-Louis, Brad Dechter, Angus Fletcher, Jacob Goldstein, Kory Mathewson, Lord Brennan of Canton, Steven Marche, Kubilay Uner, M. B. Gordy, Mark Phillips, Alan Menken, Lenny Beer, Dom Flemons, George Dyson, Michele Darling, Michael Strickland, Manny Marroquin, and my wife were kind enough to read early drafts.

Joe Pan's advice on the contract got me to the finish line.

Chris Medinger '98 gave me his boat to live on when I moved to LA. Thanks to him, his wife Grace, and their two amazing daughters who, I'm proud to say, call me Uncle Lucas.

The Bachlers of Winona, Minnesota, put me up in their home when I needed a few weeks away to work.

ACKNOWLEDGMENTS

Joie Davidow did the first professional edit of this book and her contribution made it possible to get it to the finish line.

Julia (Ivy Agusta) Henry, has been one of my closet friends since day one in Los Angeles. She's the reason I was commissioned to write a piece for SoftBank. She's a total badass.

My partners in crime and coconspirators in various endeavors are listed here. Ajay Kapur, Andrew Yarovenko, Annemarie Gaillard, Anthony Achille, Becca Nelson, Ben Dillenberger (Go Dodgers!), Caley Chase, Chris Woods, Cira Limoli Nisco, Dan Martinez, Daniel Ibri (+Joy), Denzil Thomas, Edy Lan, Gérôme Vanherf, Heather Rafter, Jayna Zweiman, Jeremy Pion-Berlin, Joe Lyske, Karim Fanous, Laura Jackman, Lonny Friedman, Mark Isham, Matt Kappel, Milo Segal, Nicole de la Torriente, Peter Rotter, P. T. Navarro, Rachael Lyske, Randy Christopher, Ryan Little, Santiago Ramones, Scott Schreer, Tio Nestor, Tomer Elbaz, Zach Dellinger, Trygge Toven, J. B. Thiebaut, Heather Rafter, Ken Miller.

To my friends and family, and friends who are like family: Angus Christopher Lowther Malcomson, Ben Cooper '99, Brittney Crystal '99, Chris Peters, Creighton Lee '99, Eugenio Casillas Rodrîguez, Irad Brandt, Jacqueline Marshall, Jean Tariech, Jesse Cameron Alick, Jessica Sarles-Dinsick, Josh and Hannah Powell, Katie Geatches, Kenneth Judy '99, Kimberlee Geatches, Mark Goldberg '99, Matt Dinsick, Matt Fowler '99 (who flew to London for the premier of the Unfinished), Michael Cohen, Nolan Frank, Raj Naidu '99, Russ Choma '99, Sarah Stevenson '99, Todd Geatches, Kimberlee Geatches,

Tommy Pace '99, Vincent Mentry, Zach Crowley '99, Zach Smith '99. I have too many aunts, uncles, and cousins to name. Thank you all!

Finally, I want to acknowledge Ben Powell. He introduced me to my wife. He introduced me to many of the people acknowledged above, and he was the finest musician I have ever known. As if that weren't enough, he was also an accomplished pilot and would fly himself to gigs and recording sessions all over the country. After a life of achievement, purpose, and meaning that would fill a man of any age with justifiable pride, Ben gracefully made his exit from this world after a battle with cancer. He was thirty-eight years old. His legacy is secure in his contribution to countless recorded musical works, the friends and family who will never forget his brilliance and charm, and his young daughter. The music of the world is a bit softer, and not as sweet, without him.

INDEX

Abbey Road Studios, 120, 133, 134, 136, 137
abductive reasoning, 108, 109–10, 152
Abelard, Peter, 196–201, 202, 203, 218, 223
Academy Awards, 36, 37
"Adieu mes amours" (song), 166
"Adore the sound" (theory), 13, 17
AI winter, 112
algorithms, 105–7, 127, 229
"All Along the Watchtower" (song), 160
"All of Me" (song), 5
Alphabet (company), 106–7
Amadeus (movie), 91
American Society of Composers, Authors, and Publishers (ASCAP), 119, 176
Apollo (deity), 9

artificial general intelligence (AGI), 87–8
artificial intelligence (AI)
origins of, 7–8, 32, 86, 87–8, 98, 99
differing views on, 7, 58, 95, 111, 141, 183, 185
creativity and, 7, 32–3, 58, 78, 86, 93–4, 104, 121–2, 128, 130, 216, 230
consciousness and, 4, 8, 32, 93–5, 97–102, 110, 151–2, 228
limitations of, 109–11, 115, 232
movie trailers and, 86–7
online media and, 104–8
Turing Tests and, 100–1, 111, 113–115
Asimov, Isaac, 152
"Ave Maria" (song), 90

Bach, Johann Sebastian, 89–90, 115–16, 182–3, 207
Bannister, Rosie, 124, 130, 131, 133, 137, 140, 141, 143
Baroque period, 91, 115
base sixty math, 156
Bayreuth Festpielhaus, 210, 213–14
Beatles, the, 170
Beethoven, Ludwig van, 2, 88, 89, 91, 215, 229
Bible, the, 155, 163–4, 201, 233
Big Bang, 187–8
Bingen, Hildegard von, 161, 162, 165, 183, 201–4, 208, 218, 220, 223
birdsong, 33–4
BMG (label), 82
bone flute, 33–5, 40, 64–5, 150–1, 169, 183
Boomwhackers, 15–16, 18–19, 190
Borges, Jorge Louis, 126, 216

Boston Dynamics, 4–6
Boxall, Andy, 137–8, 139, 150, 193
Brave (album), 181–2, 186
British Library, 162
Brontze Format, 125, 132, 145
Brown, Clifford, 222
Buckley, Jeff, 138, 160, 176, 189, 192–3, 194, 217
Buffalo Sabres, 190

Cadogan Hall, 137, 142, 144
"Calamities of Peter Abelard, The" (letter), 199
Cambrian Explosion, 174, 184
Cantor, Allison, 6, 104
Cantor, Frank, 189–91
Carafa, Fabrizio, Duke, 205
CBS Records, 189, 193
Cervantes, Miguel De, 217, 219, 220
chromaticism, 20–1, 26, 158–9, 207, 224
Cohen, Leonard, 138, 160, 176, 188–9, 192–3, 194, 223
Cold Case (TV show), 53
"Computing and Machine Intelligence" (paper), 102
consciousness, 95–8

Cope, David, 116
copyist role, 45, 126, 133
cuneiform writing, 195

"Dan Judenthum in der Musik" (essay), *see* "Jewishness in Music"
d'Arezzo, Guido, 158–9, 161, 165, 169, 183, 232
d'Avalos, Donna Maria, 204, 205–6
Dechter, Brad, 134, 145
deductive reasoning, 26, 103–5, 107–8
Dennett, Daniel, 187
digital audio workstations (DAWs), 57–60, 64, 132
Digital Trends (magazine), 138
disco music, 170, 173
DNA, 55, 177–8
    as a metaphor for musical notation, 26, 160–1, 174
Don Quixote (book), 217, 219
Donaldson, Lou, 222
Duffin, Ross, 27
Dylan, Bob, 160

Eastwood Scoring Stage, 38–9
Edison, Thomas, 78, 95, 166–8, 174–5, 180

Egyptian innovations, 12, 61, 156, 158, 200
Eighth Symphony (Schubert)
    origins of, 41, 90, 128, 226
    author's commission to complete, 3, 6, 7, 118, 124, 228–9
    role of AI in completing, 32, 93, 108, 127–32, 173, 150, 153, 193, 232
    rehearsals at Abbey Road, 133–7
    first performance, 137–8, 141, 142–6, 148–50
    responses to, 117, 138, 139–41, 142–3, 147, 152
Einstein, Albert, 94, 225
electronic dance music (EDM), 81
EMI (computer), 116, 118
Emmy Awards, 1, 36, 37, 45
Enlightenment, 165
Eno, Brian, 40
Epicurus, 96
equal temperament, 26, 27, 70, 74
Evangelical Christianity, 188, 194, 195
"Everybody Wants to Rule the World" (song), 82–5, 133

INDEX

"Everything is number" (theory), 13, 18, 94, 153, 226, 228

Feinstein, Dianne, 177
"Fly Me to the Moon" (song), 64
Ford, Jon, 181; *see also* JOYRYDE
Foreman, Milos, 91
French Revolution, 23
Fulbert of Notre Dame, 198–9

Gallant, Julian, 137
Garrihy, Andrew, 142
General Electric Company, 167
Generative Pretrained Transformer (GPT) models, 115, 151
Gershwin, George, 181–2, 183, 185, 186
Gesemkuntswerk, 210
Gesualdo, Carlo, 204–8, 218, 220, 224
Gewandhaus orchestra, 90
Ghaffari, Earl, 43
Ghosthorse, Tiokasin, 28–9, 30–1, 32, 158, 218
"Gimme a Break" (song), 52
God, Human, Animal, Machine (book), 99
Goethe, Johann Wolfgang von, 212
Golden Records, 24–5, 27–8

"Golden Verses" (work), 11, 13
Google DeepMind, 116
Google Maps, 117
Goostman, Eugene, 112–14, 169
Gordy, M. B., 74
GPS systems, 117
Grammy Awards, 36, 84
Grand Opera, 216
Greek philosophy, 12, 65, 203
Grierson, Mick, 118–19, 121, 122, 123–4, 125, 153
Groves, Leslie, General, 91–2
Guidonian Hand, 158–9, 203; *see also* d'Arezzo, Guido
Gutenberg, Johannes, 162–5, 168, 201

"Hallelujah" (song), 138, 160, 176, 187–94, 196, 203
Harmonice Musices Odhecaton (anthology), 166
Haydn, Joseph, 88, 90
Heloise of Argenteuil, 197–8, 199
Hendrix, Jimi, 160, 170
Heraclitus, 98
"Here Comes the Bride" (song), 213
Herkelmann, Arne, 142
Herodotus, 11

Hildegard, *see* Bingen, Hildegard von
Hitler, Adolf, 210, 214, 216
Hope, Elmo, 220–3, 224
How Equal Temperament Ruined Music (book), 27
Howard, Bert, 64
Huawei, 124–5, 130–1, 132, 134, 142, 145, 150
Hubbard, L. Ron, 11
Huffington, Arianna, 6
Hunger Games, The (movie franchise), 84–5

Imitation Game, 110–11; *see also* Turing Test
"Imperial March" (movie theme), 209
inductive reasoning, 26, 31, 103, 108
itinerant distance, 21–2, 24, 70

Jackson, Michael, 63, 89, 207
jazz, 36, 173, 178, 220–2
Jefferson, Geoffrey, 100–1, 102
Jesus Christ, 11, 99–100
"Jewishness in Music" (essay), 211, 213, 216
Ji, Walter, 141–2, 143, 144, 148, 150, 189

241

Johnson, Edward, 167
Jones, Quincy, 63–4
Joseph II, Emperor, 91
Josquin des Prez, 166
JOYRYDE, 181–2
Judaism, 162, 211, 213

Kelly, Dom, 135, 146
Klass, Myleene, 142, 143
Kliesch, Kevin, 41
Krakauer, Jon, 11
Kurzweil, Ray, 14, 15, 152

Labyrinths (book), 216–17
Lakota language, 28–9, 33, 158
Laplace, Pierre-Simon, 226–8
Laplace's Demon, 226, 227, 228
Larson, Erik J., 110
Larson, Steve, 115–16
Legend, John, 4
leitmotifs, 209
Levine, Michael A., 52–54, 57, 67–8, 82, 83
  DAW setup of, 67–8
library music, 118–20, 121, 123, 135
Lichtenstein, Roy, 137
Lister Medal, 101
Loebner, Hugh, 111–12
Lohengrin (opera), 213
Long Short-Term Memory (LSTM), 32, 127

Lorde, 82–3, 84–5, 123, 133
Los Alamos research labs, 92, 122
Ludwig II, King, 213

Ma, Yo-Yo, 231
Mac OS, 67
madrigal form, 204–5, 207–8
magic tricks, 113–14
Magritte, René, 17
Manchester Mark 1 computer, 101
Master, the, *see* Pythagoras
Mate 20 Pro phone launch, 124–6; *see also* Huawei
Maxamillian II, King, 213
"Menace of Mechanical Music, The" (article), 175–6
Menard, Pierre (character), 126–7, 216–17, 219, 220, 224
Mendelssohn, Felix, 90, 192, 211–13
Mendelssohn, Moses, 211
Menken, Alan, 36–7, 41, 43, 45, 46, 49–50, 63, 87, 121, 141
Mesopotamian innovations, 65, 155–6, 158, 195, 233
Meyerbeer, Giacomo, 171, 215–16, 223

Microsoft Windows, 67
Mid-Atlantic accent, 75–6
MIDI, 72, 131–2
Midsummer Night's Dream, A (play), 213
Mind (journal), 102
Monteverdi, Claudio, 208
Monty Python's Flying Circus (TV show), 175
"Moro Lasso" (libretto), 207
movie trailer music, 79–88, 104, 108–9, 119, 121, 214, 230
Mozart, Wolfgang Amadeus, 2, 88–9, 91, 212, 215, 230
"Music of the Spheres," 13, 18
musical notation, 59, 65–6, 153, 160–1, 165, 183, 232
  technology and, 131, 132, 173–4
Musk, Elon, 14–15, 152
Myth of Artificial Intelligence, The (book), 110

NASA, 24–5, 27
natural temperament, 26–7
Nazism, 214–15, 223
NBC Sports, 36
Neolithic times, 34–5
neural networks, 98–9

INDEX

Neuralink, 15
New Faces, New Sounds (album), 222
New York Times (newspaper), 168
Newton, Isaac, 225, 227
Nielsen, 106
Nuremberg rallies, 210
Nutcracker Suite (ballet), 171

Ogas, Ogi, 109
O'Gieblyn, Meghan, 99
Olympic Games broadcasts, 1, 36, 37
OpenAI (company), 116
orchestra contractor role, 43, 47
Ordo Virtutum (play), 202

Petrucci, Ottaviano, 165–6
Phaedrus (work), 61
"Philosophical Essay on Probabilities, A" (essay), 226–7
Phonograph technology, 167–70, 171–2, 174, 180, 184
"Pierre Menard, Author of the Quixote" (story), 216–17
Pink Floyd, 170
pitch, 15–16, 18–19, 33, 158
Pius IV, Pope, 204
Plato, 11, 14, 61, 95–6, 161

Playter, Robert, 4, 71, 80
plectrum banjo, 75
popular music, 75, 170, 172
Posner, Michael, 60
Pro Tools (software), 34, *see also* digital audio workstations
Pythagoras of Samos life of, 9–11
theories of, 10–16, 18–21, 24, 94, 100, 153, 217, 226, 228

Queen (band), 170
Quixote, The (fictitious work), 217, 224

Ravel, Maurice, 64
Red Consultancy, 124, 126, 130, 133, 134
Remote Control Productions, 51–2, 54, 57, 67, 71, 73, 121, 193
Renaissance period, 12, 165
Rienzi (opera), 211
Rogers, Susan, 109
Roman innovations, 157
Rosamunde (play), 131
Rosenwinkel, Kurt, 221
Rube Goldberg machines, 130

Salieri, Antonio, 91, 215
sampling, 58, 60, 72–4, 119
scales, 20–1, 30, 157

Schubert, Franz
life of, 89–93, 142, 148, 172, 212, 215, 226
work and musical style, 18, 41, 90, 92, 126, 128, 143, 152–3, 229
artificial intelligence and, 126–32, 173
Scientific Revolution, 165
Shakespeare, William, 115, 213
Shrek (movie), 192, 195, 223
Shurkin, Peter, 82–3, 85, 108
Sinatra, Frank, 63, 64, 75
Singularity, 99
Small's (club), 221
Smith, Joseph, 11
Socrates, 61
SoftBank, 5, 6
solipsism, 102
"Somewhere Over the Rainbow" (song), 16
Son, Masayoshi, 5–6
sonata form, 181–2, 230
sonic signatures, 109
Sousa, John Phillip, 175–6
Spot Robot, 4–6, 7, 110
Spotify, 105, 174
spotting sessions, 45
Stanley Cup, 45, 190, 191
Staples, Ed, 124–5

243

streaming technology, 103–4, 174, 177, 185
Sybil of the Rhine, *see* Bingen, Hildegard von
Sumerian people, 158
Super Bowl broadcasts, 1
symphonic form, 2, 128, 228–9
Symphony in C Major (Wagner), 212

Tangled (score), 37, 121
  recording of, 39–50, 136, 141
Tchaikovsky, Pyotr Ilyich, 171
Tears for Fears, 82
technology and music-making, 59, 63–8, 69, 73, 86–8, 103, 104, 122–3, 173, 183, 184–6
temperament, *see* tuning
Telephone and Phonograph Show, 167–8, 170
Thamus, King, 61, 62, 76
The Terminator (movie), 152
Theuth (deity), 61, 67, 77, 159, 175, 200
This Is What It Sounds Like (book), 109
Thomas, Denzil, 125, 126, 131, 132
"Thought Experiment Infinity" (piece), 187–8
"Thriller" (song), 207
time and time zones, 21–3, 156–8, 226
  rail travel and, 22–3, 25, 69
Today Show, The (TV show), 117
trailers, *see* movie trailers
tuning, 23–27
Turing, Alan, 92, 100–2, 110, 122
Turing Tests, 110–13, 114, 115, 151

"Unfinished," *see* Eighth Symphony (Schubert)
US Open tennis tournament, 45

Varèse, Edgard, 187
Various Positions (album), 189, 193
Vienna, 90–1, 92–3
virtual instruments, 57–9, 60–1, 66, 72, 74
Voyager space mission, 24

Wall Street Journal (newspaper), 5
Wagner, Richard, 171, 172, 208–16, 217, 220
  antisemitism and, 210–11, 213, 216, 223
Walking Dead, The (TV show), 146
Ward, Jacob, 117, 184
Warner Bros. Studios, 38–9, 45–6, 54
Western music, 18–20, 26–7, 30, 67, 115, 158–9
WeWork, 5
Who, the, 170
Wolf, Frank, 42
Wonder, Stevie, 89
World War II, 91–2

Yetnikoff, Walter, 189, 193
YouTube, 105–7

Zimmer, Hans, 51, 52, 73, 80, 123
  use of new technology, 60–61, 64, 70–1, 77